Breaking Chains, Building Bridges:

Womanism's Battle with Religious Oppression

Chapter 1: Womanism Unveiled: Navigating Intersectional Feminism

Introduction

Prepare to embark on an enlightening journey that uncovers the intricate relationship between womanism and religion. We're about to explore pivotal moments from history, ancient tales from mythological traditions, well-documented insights from peer-reviewed studies, and verified facts that come together to shape this compelling narrative. From pivotal historical events that shifted cultural paradigms to captivating mythological stories that have endured the test of time, and from well-researched studies that shed light on the interplay between these forces to indisputable facts that reveal the connections, we'll traverse a landscape of thought that invites us to challenge assumptions, question norms, and embrace the complexities of the shared human experience. Get ready to uncover a rich tapestry of insight, woven from the threads of our past and present.

Highlighting the profound significance of intersectionality within feminist discourse, we witness a transformative shift that acknowledges the intricate interconnections between various aspects of identity and experience. This framework recognizes that gender is just one thread in the complex tapestry of human existence, interwoven with factors like race, ethnicity, socioeconomic background, and sexuality. By embracing intersectionality, feminist discourse becomes more inclusive and authentic, shedding light on the distinct challenges faced by different groups. It empowers us to advocate for a more equitable world that takes into account the multifaceted realities of individuals across diverse walks of life.

At the heart of this chapter lies a crucial exploration: understanding the fundamental principles and objectives that underpin womanism. We embark on a journey to unravel the essence of womanism, a social and ideological movement that seeks to address the unique struggles faced by Black women while also advocating for gender equality and justice for all. By delving into its core tenets, we illuminate how womanism weaves together the intersections of race, gender, class, and culture. Through this lens, we gain insight into womanism's commitment to uplifting marginalized voices, fostering solidarity, and creating spaces of empowerment. As we dive deeper, we uncover a nuanced framework that challenges traditional feminism and presents a holistic vision for social transformation.

Defining Womanism

The term "womanism" found its roots in the creative mind of the renowned author, poet, and activist, Alice Walker. In 1983, Walker introduced this term to the world through her collection of essays titled "In Search of Our Mothers' Gardens: Womanist Prose." The term "womanist" was coined by Walker to address the limitations she observed within mainstream feminism, which often failed to fully encompass the experiences of Black women and other women of color.

Alice Walker's creation of the term was a response to the need for a broader framework that acknowledged the unique challenges faced by Black women. She wanted to capture the essence of a movement that celebrated their cultural heritage, strength, and resilience while addressing the interconnected systems of oppression they encountered. The term "womanist" draws inspiration from the Southern African American vernacular where "womanish" implies a sense of independence and determination.

Alice Walker's concept of womanism invites individuals to recognize and celebrate the struggles and triumphs of Black women, acknowledging their historical and cultural contributions. It encourages solidarity among women of all backgrounds while giving prominence to the experiences and perspectives that had been marginalized in earlier feminist narratives. Through her visionary creation, Walker not only coined a term but sparked a movement that continues to inspire critical dialogue, social transformation, and the celebration of diverse voices.

The distinction between womanism and feminism is essential for understanding how these two ideologies differ in their approach to addressing gender and social justice issues. While both movements share a commitment to achieving gender equality and challenging patriarchal norms, they diverge in their scope, focus, and inclusivity.

- **Scope and Inclusivity:**
- **Feminism:** Traditional feminism primarily originated in Western contexts and often centered on the experiences of white, middle-class women. While it has evolved over time to be more inclusive, early feminist movements sometimes struggled to fully address the concerns of women of color, working-class women, and those from different cultural backgrounds.
- **Womanism:** Womanism, coined by Alice Walker, emerged as a response to the limitations of feminism in encompassing the experiences of Black women and other women of color. Womanism acknowledges the intersections of race, class, and culture, making it more inclusive and attuned to the unique struggles faced by marginalized communities.
- **Cultural and Historical Context:**
- **Feminism:** Traditional feminism is deeply rooted in Western thought and often framed within the context of Euro-American history and perspectives. It has undergone multiple waves, each addressing specific issues related to women's rights and representation.
- **Womanism:** Womanism originated within the context of the African American community and draws inspiration from African American cultural experiences and traditions. It emphasizes the historical and cultural narratives of Black

women while acknowledging the ways in which race, gender, and class intersect.

- **Emphasis on Intersectionality:**
- **Feminism:** While contemporary feminism acknowledges the importance of intersectionality, some earlier forms of feminism failed to fully consider the ways in which various forms of oppression intersected, particularly those faced by women of color, LGBTQ+ individuals, and marginalized communities.
- **Womanism:** Intersectionality is a foundational aspect of womanism. It recognizes the interconnectedness of different forms of oppression and how they impact individuals differently based on their identities. Womanism insists on addressing these intersections to create more holistic and accurate solutions.
- **Concept of Liberation:**
- **Feminism:** Feminism seeks to liberate women from patriarchal norms, aiming to level the playing field in various social, economic, and political spheres.
- **Womanism:** Womanism expands beyond the liberation of women to encompass the well-being and empowerment of entire communities. It emphasizes a collective struggle for justice and liberation, addressing issues that extend beyond gender alone.

While feminism and womanism both advocate for gender equality and social justice, womanism stands out for its intersectional approach that accounts for race, class, culture, and other factors. It serves as a response to the limitations of traditional feminism and strives to create a more inclusive and holistic understanding of the struggles faced by women in diverse contexts.

At the heart of womanism lies a profound commitment to amplifying the voices and experiences of Black women and other marginalized groups. Unlike traditional feminism, which at times centered on the perspectives of white, middle-class women, womanism emerges as a potent response to the need for a more inclusive and intersectional approach.

Womanism recognizes that the experiences of Black women are shaped not only by gender but also by race, class, culture, and historical context. It acknowledges the complexities of their lives – the overlapping oppressions they face – and seeks to address these interconnected challenges.

In the realm of womanism, the narratives, struggles, and triumphs of Black women take center stage. It shines a light on their resilience in the face of adversity, their contributions to history and culture, and their agency in creating change. By emphasizing the experiences of Black women, womanism exposes the limitations of previous feminist movements that failed to fully capture the diversity of women's lives.

Yet, womanism goes beyond race and gender. It extends its embrace to include other marginalized groups, recognizing the intersections of identities and the shared struggles that arise. This inclusive approach enriches the movement, creating a space where individuals can unite under the banner of justice, equity, and empowerment.

By focusing on the experiences of Black women and marginalized groups, womanism expands the narrative of feminism. It challenges us to recognize the nuances of lived experiences, break down barriers, and build bridges of understanding. Through womanism, we embrace the strength that comes from unity, solidarity, and the collective journey toward a more just and inclusive world.

Intersectionality as a Foundational Concept

Intersectionality is a dynamic concept that recognizes the multifaceted nature of identity and how various forms of oppression intersect and interact. It highlights the fact that individuals are not defined solely by a single aspect of their identity, such as gender, but rather by the complex interplay of multiple identities, including race, class, sexuality, disability, and more. This term, coined by Kimberlé Crenshaw, underscores the need to address overlapping systems of discrimination and privilege that shape people's experiences.

In the context of womanist thought, intersectionality is not just a theoretical concept; it's a foundational pillar. Womanism acknowledges that the struggles faced by Black women are not isolated incidents of sexism or racism, but the result of a complex web of social dynamics. By recognizing and exploring these intersections, womanism provides a lens through which to fully comprehend the layered nature of oppression.

Womanism's relevance to intersectionality stems from its commitment to understanding the totality of an individual's identity and experiences. It rejects the tendency to address issues in isolation and insists on viewing them through an interconnected lens. This approach allows womanism to be more inclusive, addressing the concerns of marginalized groups that may be sidelined by other feminist perspectives.

Furthermore, intersectionality within womanism acknowledges that liberation is not a one-size-fits-all solution. The unique challenges faced by individuals based on their specific intersections require tailored approaches. By embracing intersectionality, womanism amplifies the voices and experiences of those who have been historically silenced or marginalized.

In essence, intersectionality is the heartbeat of womanist thought. It reminds us that our identities and experiences are layered, and our struggles are interconnected. Womanism's commitment to intersectionality is a testament to its authenticity and dedication to addressing the complex realities of individuals' lives, advocating for justice, and creating space for all voices to be heard.

The concept of intersecting identities underscores the intricate and often nuanced ways in which various aspects of an individual's identity come together to shape their experiences, opportunities, and challenges. These identities can include factors such as race, gender, class, sexuality, ethnicity, religion, and more. Rather than existing in isolation, these identities intersect and interact, leading to unique lived experiences that can differ significantly from those of individuals with different combinations of identities.

For example, a Black woman's experience will be distinct from that of a white woman or a Black man due to the intersection of race and gender. Similarly, an LGBTQ+ person's experience might be influenced by their sexual orientation and the cultural context they belong to. These intersections often lead to compounded forms of discrimination, as individuals face biases that arise from the convergence of multiple marginalized identities.

The impact of intersecting identities can manifest in various ways:

- **Marginalization:** Individuals with intersecting marginalized identities can experience greater levels of marginalization and exclusion due to the compounded effects of discrimination.
- **Privilege and Oppression:** On the flip side, intersecting identities can also grant certain privileges, making it important to recognize how an individual's experiences might differ based on their various identities.
- **Access to Resources:** Intersecting identities can influence an individual's access to education, healthcare, job opportunities, and other resources. Those with multiple marginalized identities might encounter additional barriers.
- **Representation and Visibility:** Intersectionality impacts how different groups are represented and acknowledged within society. The experiences of individuals with less visible identities may be overlooked or ignored.
- **Cultural Context:** The way intersecting identities are perceived can vary across cultures and regions. This adds complexity to an individual's experiences, as they navigate different societal expectations and norms.

Recognizing the impact of intersecting identities is essential for understanding the complexity of individuals' lives and crafting inclusive policies, social movements, and dialogue. It also underscores the importance of amplifying voices that have historically been silenced and advocating for justice that addresses these intersecting forms of discrimination. In the realm of womanism, intersectionality is not just a theoretical concept but a lived reality that shapes the movement's goals, actions, and advocacy.

Intersectionality serves as a powerful lens through which womanist thought critically analyzes the role of religion in shaping the lives of individuals with intersecting identities. When applied to the study of religion, intersectionality reveals the intricate ways in which systems of faith and spirituality intersect with race, gender, class, and other facets of identity. This intersectional perspective provides deeper insights into how religion both informs and impacts the lives of individuals within the womanist framework.

- **Understanding Complex Belonging:** Intersectionality acknowledges that individuals don't belong to a singular identity group. In womanist analyses of religion, this means recognizing how people's religious beliefs and practices intersect with their racial, gender, and socioeconomic identities. This understanding adds complexity to their relationship with faith, as they navigate the intersections of various dimensions of self.
- **Challenging Dual Marginalization:** Womanist analyses using an intersectional approach uncover how religion can either exacerbate or challenge dual marginalization. For instance, Black women might experience marginalization within both their faith communities and society at large due to their intersecting identities. Womanist thought critically assesses how religious spaces can either reinforce or resist this dual marginalization.
- **Recognizing Cultural and Historical Contexts:** Intersectionality prompts womanist scholars to examine religion within its cultural and historical contexts. By understanding how different identities have been historically marginalized or privileged, they can analyze how religious practices and interpretations have perpetuated or challenged these power dynamics.
- **Unveiling Power Structures:** Womanist analyses informed by intersectionality highlight the power structures within religious institutions. They reveal how gender, race, and other identities influence access to leadership roles, decision-making, and the interpretation of religious texts. This scrutiny informs discussions about equity and justice within religious settings.

- **Unmasking Liberation Possibilities:** Intersectionality uncovers the potential for liberation and empowerment within religious spaces. By acknowledging the diverse identities within religious communities, womanist analyses explore how these identities can be sources of strength, resistance, and solidarity in the face of oppression.
- **Empowering Inclusive Theology:** Intersectional analyses inform womanist efforts to shape more inclusive theological narratives. By acknowledging the intersections of oppression and resilience, womanist scholars contribute to the development of theological frameworks that empower marginalized groups and challenge hierarchical norms.

In essence, intersectionality informs womanist analyses of religion by uncovering the complex ways that faith intersects with other dimensions of identity. It helps illuminate the often-overlooked narratives of marginalized individuals within religious contexts, enriching womanism's insights into the dual role of religion in both shaping and undermining the lives of those it touches.

Womanist Aims and Principles

The objectives of womanism encompass a holistic vision that extends beyond gender equity, addressing the interconnected challenges of racial justice and social transformation. These objectives are interwoven, reflecting the multidimensional approach of womanist thought. Here's an outline highlighting these key objectives:

I. Gender Equity:

- Recognition of Women's Agency: Womanism emphasizes the agency, autonomy, and empowerment of women, including marginalized groups often excluded from mainstream feminist narratives.
- Challenging Patriarchy: Womanist thought confronts patriarchal norms and structures that perpetuate gender-based inequalities, advocating for a more balanced power dynamic between genders.

- Inclusive Feminism: Womanism strives for a feminism that recognizes and celebrates the diversity of women's experiences, ensuring that gender equity is not achieved at the expense of other identities.

II. Racial Justice:

- Addressing Intersectionality: Womanism places a spotlight on the intersection of race and gender, recognizing the unique struggles faced by Black women and women of color.
- Confronting Racism: Womanism actively challenges racism within both society and institutions, advocating for racial justice and equity for all marginalized communities.
- Centering Marginalized Voices: Womanist objectives include amplifying the voices and narratives of marginalized groups, particularly Black women, whose experiences have been historically marginalized.

III. Social Transformation:

- Collectivism and Community: Womanism emphasizes the importance of collective action, encouraging collaboration and solidarity among diverse groups for the purpose of social change.
- Disrupting Norms: Womanist thought seeks to disrupt societal norms that perpetuate oppression, encouraging critical thinking and creative strategies to challenge the status quo.
- Liberation of All: Womanism envisions a world where the liberation of all individuals—regardless of their identity—is achieved, dismantling systems of oppression that hinder this goal.

IV. Embracing Cultural Authenticity:

- Valuing Cultural Heritage: Womanism celebrates cultural heritage and traditions, recognizing the unique contributions and wisdom of different communities.
- Rejecting Assimilation: Womanism challenges the pressure to assimilate into dominant cultural norms and encourages the celebration of diverse cultural expressions.

V. Fostering Inclusive Spirituality:

- Reimagining Spirituality: Womanism calls for a spirituality that honors the sacredness of life, reframing traditional religious narratives to be more inclusive and empowering.
- Challenging Religious Oppression: Womanism confronts religious institutions and interpretations that perpetuate gender and racial-based oppression, aiming for transformative change.

In essence, womanism's objectives encompass a profound commitment to creating a more just, equitable, and inclusive society. By simultaneously addressing gender equity, racial justice, and social transformation, womanism presents a framework that acknowledges the complexities of human experiences and advocates for a more interconnected and liberated world.

Womanist ethics and spirituality stand as central components of the womanist framework, shaping its principles and guiding its pursuit of justice, liberation, and holistic well-being. These components are intertwined, reflecting the interconnected nature of womanist thought. Let's delve into these aspects:

1. Womanist Ethics:

- **Rooted in Lived Experience:** Womanist ethics draw inspiration from the lived experiences of Black women and marginalized groups. It recognizes that moral principles are shaped by the realities individuals face daily.
- **Caring for Community:** Womanist ethics emphasize communal care and interconnectedness. This care extends beyond individual well-being to encompass the collective, fostering a sense of responsibility for the betterment of all.
- **Centering Justice:** Justice is a cornerstone of womanist ethics. It involves not only addressing individual harm but dismantling oppressive systems and advocating for equitable social structures.
- **Challenging Hierarchies:** Womanist ethics challenge hierarchies that perpetuate oppression. It questions power dynamics that marginalize certain identities, striving for a more inclusive and equitable world.

- **Ethics of Resistance:** Womanist ethics are deeply rooted in resistance to injustice. It recognizes that defying oppressive norms is an ethical imperative, often requiring courageous and transformative actions.

2. Womanist Spirituality:

- **Honoring Ancestry:** Womanist spirituality pays homage to ancestral wisdom, traditions, and cultural heritage. It recognizes the spirituality that emerges from the experiences of Black women and marginalized communities.
- **Reclaiming Narrative:** Womanist spirituality seeks to reclaim and reshape religious narratives. It dismantles harmful interpretations that perpetuate oppression, allowing individuals to reconnect with their spirituality authentically.
- **Liberation Theology:** Womanist spirituality often aligns with liberation theology, advocating for the liberation of all oppressed individuals. It envisions a spirituality that actively works towards social justice and freedom.
- **Communion with the Sacred:** Womanist spirituality embraces the sacredness of everyday life and uplifts the spiritual connections present in various aspects of existence, including relationships, creativity, and social change.
- **Holistic Well-Being:** Womanist spirituality recognizes the interdependence of mind, body, and spirit. It prioritizes holistic well-being and encourages practices that nourish all dimensions of self.

Both womanist ethics and spirituality provide the framework for transformative action and introspection. Womanism's ethics guide individuals to challenge oppressive structures, center justice, and care for marginalized communities. Simultaneously, its spirituality offers a way to heal, reclaim agency, and engage in practices that honor diverse cultural expressions and interconnectedness. Together, these components weave a tapestry of thought and action that drives womanism's commitment to liberation, equity, and the creation of a more just world.

The womanist commitment to inclusive and holistic liberation embodies a profound dedication to achieving freedom, equity, and well-being for all individuals, particularly those who have been historically marginalized or oppressed. This commitment goes beyond a singular focus on gender or race and instead recognizes the interconnected nature of oppression and privilege across various identities.

1. Intersectional Liberation: Womanism embraces the concept of intersectionality, acknowledging that people's identities are multifaceted and intertwined. Inclusive liberation means recognizing how different forms of oppression intersect and impact individuals' lives uniquely. Womanism seeks to liberate individuals from the chains of racism, sexism, classism, homophobia, and other forms of discrimination simultaneously.

2. Embracing Diversity: The commitment to inclusive liberation involves celebrating the diverse experiences and perspectives of individuals. Womanism values the rich tapestry of identities, cultures, and histories that contribute to the collective human experience. It rejects any attempt to achieve liberation at the expense of other marginalized groups.

3. Challenging Systemic Oppression: Holistic liberation requires confronting the systemic structures that perpetuate oppression. Womanism advocates for dismantling unjust systems and challenging the power dynamics that maintain inequality. This involves not only addressing individual instances of injustice but also striving to transform the very foundations of society.

4. Healing and Empowerment: Inclusive and holistic liberation entails healing from the wounds of oppression and reclaiming agency. Womanism recognizes the importance of emotional, psychological, and spiritual well-being as integral to true liberation. It encourages individuals to engage in self-care practices that nourish their overall health.

5. Collective Action: Womanism emphasizes the power of collective action in achieving liberation. It recognizes that no single individual can be free until all are free. This commitment to solidarity drives collaboration and alliances across diverse communities to challenge oppressive structures and promote justice.

6. Liberation of the Whole Self: Holistic liberation encompasses the liberation of the whole self – mind, body, spirit, and identity. Womanism rejects compartmentalization and encourages individuals to embrace their full authenticity, including cultural heritage, spirituality, and personal growth.

In essence, womanism's commitment to inclusive and holistic liberation reflects a profound understanding of the complexities of human experiences. It champions justice that addresses the intersections of identity and seeks to create a world where all individuals can thrive without compromising any aspect of their identity. By embracing diversity, challenging systemic oppression, and fostering healing and empowerment, womanism paves the way for a transformative journey towards liberation that encompasses the entirety of the human experience.

The Spectrum of Womanist Thought

The womanist movement is a vibrant and diverse tapestry woven from a multitude of perspectives, voices, and experiences. Its strength lies in the recognition that no single narrative can capture the entirety of the diverse lives it seeks to uplift. The diversity within womanism enriches the movement, offering a kaleidoscope of insights and understandings that collectively challenge oppressive norms and work towards justice.

1. Cultural and Ethnic Diversity: Womanism transcends geographical boundaries, encompassing the experiences of women of various racial, ethnic, and cultural backgrounds. Whether African American, Afro-Caribbean, African, Latina, Indigenous, or from other backgrounds, womanism acknowledges the nuances of identity shaped by heritage and history.

2. Class and Socioeconomic Diversity: Womanism addresses the intersection of class and socioeconomic status, recognizing that individuals within the movement come from diverse economic backgrounds. This diversity contributes to discussions about access to resources, opportunities, and the impact of economic disparities on liberation.

3. Religious and Spiritual Diversity: Within womanism, there exists a range of religious and spiritual beliefs. Womanist thought engages with diverse religious traditions, including Christianity, Islam, Indigenous spirituality, and more. This diversity allows for a nuanced exploration of how faith intersects with gender and race.

4. LGBTQ+ Inclusivity: Womanism embraces LGBTQ+ individuals and their experiences, acknowledging the intersection of gender and sexual identities. This inclusivity enriches discussions about the unique challenges faced by LGBTQ+ individuals within marginalized communities.

5. Generation and Age Diversity: Womanism transcends generations, with perspectives and concerns varying across different age groups. Younger individuals bring new insights influenced by contemporary issues, while older generations offer wisdom drawn from historical struggles and progress.

6. Academic and Activist Perspectives: The movement encompasses academics, scholars, activists, artists, and everyday individuals. This diversity of perspectives shapes the approaches taken within womanism, whether through theoretical discourse, grassroots activism, artistic expression, or community organizing.

7. Urban and Rural Perspectives: Womanism acknowledges the diverse lived experiences of those from urban and rural settings. The challenges and opportunities presented by these different environments influence the way individuals engage with womanist thought and activism.

8. Global and Diasporic Connections: Womanism is not confined to a single geographic location. It engages with the experiences of women across the African diaspora and beyond, creating global networks that celebrate shared histories and struggles.

The diversity within womanism is its strength, allowing for a multi-dimensional exploration of the complex intersections of identity, oppression, and liberation. While these perspectives may vary, they are united by a commitment to justice, equity, and the empowerment of marginalized individuals. This diversity challenges essentialism and embraces the reality that liberation is a complex journey that must honor the unique experiences of each person within the larger movement.

Variations in religious affiliations and approaches to spirituality are integral to the diverse tapestry of womanist thought. Womanism's inclusive nature embraces a wide spectrum of religious backgrounds and perspectives, reflecting the complex interplay between faith, identity, and liberation. This diversity enriches the movement by offering a multitude of ways to engage with spirituality while challenging traditional norms.

1. Intersection of Faith and Feminism: Womanism navigates the relationship between faith and feminism, acknowledging that individuals can hold diverse religious beliefs while advocating for gender equity and justice. Some womanists find alignment with their faith's teachings, while others critique religious institutions that perpetuate oppression.

2. Christian Womanism: Many womanists identify with Christianity, often seeking to reinterpret and reclaim biblical narratives that empower women and marginalized groups. Christian womanism emphasizes liberation theology, advocating for the liberation of all oppressed individuals through faith.

3. Indigenous and Ancestral Spirituality: Some womanists draw from indigenous and ancestral spiritual traditions, reconnecting with their cultural heritage to inform their activism and perspectives. This approach emphasizes a deep relationship with the land, ancestors, and nature.

4. Interfaith Exploration: Interfaith womanism transcends religious boundaries, fostering dialogue and cooperation between individuals from different faiths. It recognizes the shared struggle for justice while appreciating the distinct wisdom each tradition offers.

5. Feminist Theology: Some womanists engage in feminist theology, which critically examines religious doctrines and texts from a feminist perspective. This approach challenges patriarchal interpretations and seeks to amplify women's voices within religious traditions.

6. Humanism and Secular Womanism: For some, womanism intersects with humanism, secularism, or atheism. These perspectives emphasize critical thinking, ethics, and human rights without adherence to traditional religious beliefs.

7. LGBTQ+ Affirming Approaches: Certain womanists advocate for LGBTQ+ inclusion within religious contexts, working to create spaces that affirm the identities and experiences of LGBTQ+ individuals while challenging conservative interpretations.

8. Mysticism and Personal Experience: Some womanists explore spirituality through mysticism and personal experiences, valuing the connection between the self and the divine. This approach often prioritizes the inner journey of spiritual growth and understanding.

9. Cultural Syncretism: Cultural syncretism involves blending religious elements from various traditions. Womanists who engage in syncretism create unique spiritual practices that honor their cultural background while challenging normative religious structures.

10. Rituals and Activism: Spirituality and activism intertwine for many womanists, manifesting in rituals, ceremonies, and practices that fuel their advocacy work. These practices provide emotional sustenance and a sense of purpose.

The variations in religious affiliations and approaches to spirituality within womanism exemplify the movement's commitment to honoring diverse lived experiences. This inclusivity acknowledges the importance of individual agency in navigating faith, while collectively striving for justice, equity, and liberation. By embracing a wide array of perspectives, womanism reflects the intricate intersections of identity, spirituality, and social change.

Various womanist thinkers have made significant contributions to shaping and advancing womanist thought, enriching discussions on gender, race, spirituality, and social justice. Each thinker brings a unique perspective, adding layers of insight to the movement. Here are a few notable womanist thinkers and their key contributions:

1. Alice Walker:

- Coined the term "womanist" in her essay collection "In Search of Our Mothers' Gardens: Womanist Prose."
- Emphasized the importance of centering the experiences and struggles of Black women within feminist discourse.
- Advocated for the recognition of the spiritual and cultural wisdom passed down through generations of Black women.

2. Bell Hooks:

- Introduced the concept of "oppositional gaze," highlighting the importance of critiquing and resisting mainstream media representations.
- Addressed the intersections of race, class, and gender in her book "Ain't I a Woman?: Black Women and Feminism."
- Emphasized the need for an inclusive feminist movement that centers the experiences of all marginalized groups.

3. Audre Lorde:

- Addressed the intersections of identity, including race, gender, and sexuality, in her writing and poetry.
- Coined the term "the erotic" to encompass a sense of personal power, creativity, and self-affirmation.
- Emphasized the importance of acknowledging and celebrating differences in identity within the feminist movement.

4. Cheryl Townsend Gilkes:

- Contributed to the development of womanist theology by addressing the spiritual experiences of Black women in the church.
- Explored the ways in which Black women's religious practices and expressions challenge traditional religious norms.
- Advocated for a womanist theological framework that uplifts the unique perspectives of Black women.

5. Emilie M. Townes:

- Pioneered womanist ethics, exploring the intersections of race, gender, and sexuality within moral philosophy.
- Addressed the ethics of care, justice, and resistance within womanist thought.
- Explored the concept of "breaking bread" as a metaphor for transformative community-building and solidarity.

6. Katie Geneva Cannon:

- Contributed to womanist theology by examining the experiences of African American women within the context of Christianity.
- Emphasized the importance of addressing the historical and contemporary struggles faced by Black women in religious spaces.
- Advocated for womanist theological approaches that honor the spiritual wisdom of marginalized communities.

These womanist thinkers, among many others, have expanded the boundaries of feminist discourse by incorporating race, culture, spirituality, and intersectionality into their analyses. Their contributions have paved the way for a more inclusive and comprehensive understanding of the complexities of identity, oppression, and liberation.

Conclusion

In this chapter, we embarked on a journey into the heart of womanism, uncovering its foundational principles and objectives. We explored how womanism challenges traditional feminist narratives by centering the experiences of Black women and other marginalized groups. Intersectionality emerged as a crucial lens through which womanism addresses the complex intersections of identity, oppression, and privilege. We delved into the multifaceted components of womanism, including its ethics, spirituality, and commitment to inclusive and holistic liberation. This chapter laid the groundwork for understanding womanism's unique perspective and its dedication to dismantling systems of oppression while fostering empowerment and justice.

Preview of Upcoming Chapters: As we delve further into this exploration, upcoming chapters will cast a spotlight on the intricate relationship between religion and womanism. We will examine how religious beliefs, practices, and institutions intersect with womanist thought, both empowering and sometimes limiting its vision. These chapters will explore womanism's engagement with various religious traditions, its critiques of oppressive religious norms, and the transformative potential of faith within the movement.

Engagement with Womanism: Engaging with womanism offers a gateway to a multidimensional perspective that spans faith, social justice, and personal identity. It encourages us to challenge preconceived notions and explore the rich tapestry of experiences that shape the lives of women, especially those on the margins. As we continue this exploration, we invite you to critically examine the intersections of gender, race, spirituality, and activism. By embracing womanism's holistic approach, we embark on a journey toward understanding, empathy, and the collective pursuit of a more just and inclusive world. So, join us as we unravel the intricate threads that weave womanism into the fabric of our complex and diverse existence.

Chapter 2: Faith and Identity: The Role of Religion in Shaping Womanist Perspectives

Welcome to a chapter that delves deep into the intricate relationship between faith and womanist identities. In the previous chapters, we laid the foundation for understanding womanism's commitment to gender equity, racial justice, and holistic liberation. Now, we turn our gaze towards how these principles intersect with religious beliefs, practices, and institutions.

Faith has always been a powerful force in shaping human experiences and societies, often providing solace, guidance, and a sense of belonging. Within the context of womanism, faith takes on new dimensions as it intertwines with the lived realities of Black women and marginalized communities. This chapter invites us to explore the dynamic ways in which faith informs womanist identities, empowerment, and activism.

As we navigate this exploration, we'll uncover how womanism engages with various religious traditions, from Christianity to indigenous spirituality. We'll discuss how womanist thought critically examines religious institutions that perpetuate oppression, while also celebrating the transformative potential of faith within the movement. From reclaiming religious narratives to challenging hierarchical structures, womanism offers a lens through which faith becomes a catalyst for social change and personal growth.

The pages ahead will reveal the complexities and nuances of the relationship between faith and womanist identities. We'll encounter stories of resilience, narratives of resistance, and the beauty of diverse spiritual expressions. By understanding how faith intersects with womanism, we gain deeper insights into the intersections of gender, race, and spirituality that shape the lives of individuals on the margins. So, let's embark on this journey of discovery, where faith becomes a lens through which we witness the powerful interplay of identity, liberation, and belief.

Within the womanist movement, the tapestry of religious backgrounds is as rich and diverse as the individuals who contribute to its growth. Womanist scholars and activists hail from various religious traditions, each bringing their unique perspectives and experiences to the table. This diversity of religious backgrounds enriches the movement, showcasing how faith can intersect with gender, race, and social justice in multifaceted ways.

Christian Womanism: Many womanist thinkers are rooted in Christianity, with interpretations that challenge patriarchal norms and emphasize the stories of Black women in the Bible. They engage with liberation theology and reinterpret religious narratives through a lens of empowerment and justice.

Indigenous Spirituality: Some womanist activists draw from indigenous spiritual traditions, reconnecting with ancestral wisdom and integrating indigenous practices into their activism. This approach highlights the importance of culture, land, and community in their faith journey.

Interfaith Engagement: Womanist scholars often engage with interfaith dialogues, recognizing the shared struggle for justice across religious traditions. This approach fosters collaboration, understanding, and solidarity among individuals from diverse faith backgrounds.

Feminist Theology: Many womanist scholars incorporate feminist theology into their work, critiquing religious doctrines from a feminist perspective. They challenge patriarchal interpretations and advocate for the recognition of women's voices within religious traditions.

Secular and Humanist Perspectives: Some womanist activists align with secular or humanist perspectives, focusing on ethics, human rights, and social justice without adherence to traditional religious beliefs. This approach highlights the role of critical thinking and compassion in their activism.

LGBTQ+ Affirming Faith: Womanist thinkers often advocate for LGBTQ+ inclusion within religious spaces, interpreting faith in ways that affirm diverse sexual orientations and gender identities. This intersection challenges conservative religious interpretations.

Mystical and Personal Spirituality: Others engage with spirituality through mysticism and personal experiences, emphasizing the inner journey, personal growth, and a sense of connection with the divine.

Cultural Syncretism: Some womanists engage in cultural syncretism, blending elements of different religious traditions and cultural practices. This approach honors their heritage while challenging traditional religious structures.

Reclaiming and Reshaping: Womanists reclaim and reshape religious narratives, drawing from their unique identities and experiences to challenge oppressive norms within their faith communities.

This diverse array of religious backgrounds showcases how womanism embraces a wide spectrum of beliefs and practices. Each perspective contributes to the broader conversation about the intersection of faith, identity, and justice, reminding us that the relationship between religion and womanist identities is multi-dimensional and deeply personal.

Understanding how religious upbringing shapes worldviews within womanism is a crucial key to unlocking the complexities of individuals' identities, beliefs, and actions. Religion often plays a foundational role in shaping one's values, perspectives, and sense of self. In the context of womanism, recognizing the impact of religious upbringing sheds light on the diverse ways in which faith intersects with gender, race, and social justice.

1. Shaping Identity and Belief Systems: Religious upbringing molds an individual's identity, influencing how they see themselves and their place in the world. It informs their values, morals, and ethical compass. Within womanism, this means that the intersection of faith and identity is not just theoretical; it's deeply personal and intimately tied to an individual's upbringing.

2. Navigating Religious Norms and Expectations: Religious teachings often come with prescribed norms and expectations. Understanding how these norms intersect with gender and race is pivotal in comprehending the challenges faced by women of color within religious contexts. Womanism critically examines these norms and their impact on marginalized groups.

3. Empowerment and Resistance: Religious upbringing can be a source of empowerment and resistance. Many womanists draw strength from their faith to challenge oppressive structures and advocate for justice. Understanding how religious beliefs fuel activism provides a deeper insight into the motivations behind womanist advocacy.

4. Reclaiming and Reinterpreting: Womanism often involves reclaiming and reinterpreting religious narratives. Recognizing the influence of religious upbringing on these interpretations offers a lens through which to understand the process of reclaiming agency within faith spaces.

5. Intersections of Faith and Activism: Religious upbringing often informs an individual's approach to activism. Some womanists draw from their faith traditions to inspire social change, while others may challenge aspects of their upbringing that perpetuate oppression.

6. Healing and Well-Being: Religious upbringing can impact how individuals approach healing and well-being. For some, faith is a source of comfort and resilience, while for others, it may be associated with trauma. Understanding this relationship aids in comprehending the multifaceted ways womanists navigate their emotional and spiritual lives.

7. Diverse Interpretations: Religious upbringing leads to diverse interpretations of faith. Within womanism, understanding these interpretations fosters dialogue and mutual understanding among individuals with varying perspectives.

By recognizing the influence of religious upbringing, we gain a deeper appreciation for the intricate interplay between faith, identity, and social justice within womanism. It allows us to engage with womanist thought in a more nuanced manner, appreciating the diverse pathways individuals take as they navigate the intersections of their beliefs and the pursuit of equity and liberation.

Religion's Influence on Individual Identity

Religion plays a profound role in shaping individual identities, influencing how people perceive themselves, their place in the world, and their relationships with others. It's a powerful force that often intersects with various aspects of identity, including gender, race, culture, and more. Within the context of womanism, the role of religion in shaping identities takes on added complexity, as it intersects with the experiences of Black women and marginalized communities. Here's how religion influences individual identities:

1. Framework for Beliefs and Values: Religion provides a framework of beliefs, values, and moral principles that guide how individuals view the world. These beliefs shape one's sense of right and wrong, affecting choices and interactions with others. This framework can be a source of empowerment, fostering a sense of purpose and direction.

2. Cultural and Racial Identity: Religion often intertwines with cultural and racial identity, influencing traditions, rituals, and practices. For marginalized communities, such as Black women, religion can be a vehicle for celebrating cultural heritage and reclaiming agency in the face of historical oppression.

3. Gender Identity and Roles: Religious teachings frequently influence gender roles and expectations. In the case of womanism, understanding how religious norms intersect with gender identity is essential for recognizing the challenges and opportunities faced by women of color within faith spaces.

4. Community and Social Bonds: Religious communities provide a sense of belonging and social support. Connections formed within religious settings can significantly shape an individual's sense of community and belonging, impacting their overall well-being.

5. Intersectionality and Identity Layers: Religion intersects with other aspects of identity, creating layers of complexity. An individual's experience as a Black woman within a specific faith tradition, for instance, is informed by the interplay of race, gender, and spirituality.

6. Empowerment and Resistance: Religion can empower individuals to resist oppression and work for justice. In womanism, faith serves as a source of empowerment, motivating women to challenge systemic inequalities and reclaim their agency.

7. Navigating Cultural Norms: Religious teachings often interact with cultural norms, influencing an individual's choices and behaviors. Womanists examine these intersections to challenge harmful norms and seek authentic expressions of identity.

8. Reinterpretation and Liberation: Some individuals reinterpret religious teachings to align with their pursuit of liberation and equity. This process involves critically analyzing religious texts and traditions to challenge oppressive interpretations.

9. Spirituality and Well-Being: Religion provides a framework for spiritual practices that nurture well-being. Understanding how these practices intersect with identity helps us appreciate the diverse ways in which individuals find solace and strength.

In sum, religion is a complex web that weaves together an individual's beliefs, values, culture, and relationships. Within womanism, the role of religion in shaping identities is particularly significant, as it intersects with the experiences of those who have been marginalized and empowers them to reclaim their narratives and pursue justice.

Collective Identity and Religious Traditions

Examining Communal Religious Practices and Collective Identity: Communal religious practices hold immense significance in shaping collective womanist identities. These practices provide spaces for individuals to come together, celebrate shared beliefs, and reaffirm cultural heritage. Within these gatherings, womanists find a sense of belonging and connection, as their faith intersects with their experiences as Black women and other marginalized groups. These practices not only foster a sense of community but also serve as platforms for discussing social issues and fostering collective empowerment.

Fostering Solidarity and Resistance: Religious communities serve as hubs for solidarity and resistance within womanism. They offer platforms for marginalized individuals to unite against systemic injustices, drawing inspiration from their faith to challenge oppressive norms. Womanists find strength in shared narratives and experiences, using religious spaces as launchpads for activism and advocacy. By standing together, they amplify their voices and work towards transformative change.

Navigating Connections to Religious Traditions: Womanist thinkers navigate their connections to religious traditions with a sense of complexity and purpose. They critically engage with religious teachings, reinterpreting them through a womanist lens that centers the experiences of Black women. This process involves reclaiming narratives that have been historically marginalized and using them to empower and validate the identities of marginalized individuals. Womanist thought recognizes the potential for transformation within religious traditions, while also acknowledging the need to challenge and reshape harmful norms.

Reclaiming Agency and Voice: Religious practices provide spaces for womanists to reclaim agency and voice that may have been suppressed in other contexts. Through rituals, songs, and communal gatherings, womanists celebrate their cultural heritage and assert their right to shape religious narratives. This reclamation is essential for acknowledging the contributions of Black women and other marginalized groups to their faith traditions.

Negotiating Complex Identities: The intersection of faith and identity within womanism is complex and nuanced. Womanist thinkers often negotiate their connections to religious traditions while acknowledging the potential conflicts between patriarchal interpretations and their pursuit of liberation. This negotiation involves critical examination, reinterpretation, and the creation of alternative narratives that center the experiences of marginalized individuals.

Spiritual and Emotional Resilience: Communal religious practices offer spiritual and emotional resilience to womanist thinkers. In spaces of worship and community, they find support, healing, and a sense of purpose that sustain them in their pursuit of justice. These practices provide a space to process collective trauma and celebrate collective victories.

In conclusion, communal religious practices play a pivotal role in shaping collective womanist identities. These practices foster solidarity, resistance, and a sense of belonging within religious communities. Womanist thinkers navigate their connections to religious traditions with a nuanced approach, reclaiming agency, and reshaping narratives to align with their pursuit of justice and liberation. Through these practices, womanists celebrate their cultural heritage, challenge oppressive norms, and find strength in shared narratives of empowerment.

Religion as a Source of Empowerment

Religion has often served as a powerful source of empowerment for womanists, providing a foundation upon which they build resilience, agency, and a platform for advocating for justice. The intersection of faith and womanist identity creates spaces of empowerment that challenge systemic oppression and amplify the voices of marginalized individuals. Here are several instances where religion has been a source of empowerment for womanists:

1. Reclaiming Narratives: Religious texts and traditions have been used to suppress the voices of women and marginalized groups. However, womanists have reclaimed these narratives, interpreting them in ways that center the experiences of Black women and challenge patriarchal interpretations. This process of reclamation empowers womanists to reshape their own identities and narratives within their faith communities.

2. Connection to Ancestry: For many womanists, faith provides a connection to their ancestral heritage and the wisdom of their foremothers. By drawing inspiration from the spiritual practices of their ancestors, womanists find strength in their cultural roots, fostering a sense of continuity and pride that empowers them to navigate contemporary challenges.

3. Collective Solidarity: Religious communities offer spaces for collective solidarity and shared struggles. Womanists come together to support one another, fostering a sense of community that empowers them to face adversity and resist systemic oppression. These spaces provide validation and affirmation, reminding womanists that they are not alone in their pursuit of justice.

4. Moral Authority: Religious teachings often carry moral authority within communities. Womanists draw on these teachings to advocate for gender equity and social justice, using their faith as a platform to challenge oppressive norms and practices. By invoking the moral principles of their faith, they gain authority in advocating for change.

5. Mobilizing for Change: Religious spaces provide a platform for mobilizing and organizing for social change. Womanists harness the energy of their faith communities to address issues such as racial injustice, gender discrimination, and economic disparities. These spaces become hubs of activism, empowering womanists to take collective action.

6. Centering Healing and Wholeness: Religion can be a source of emotional and spiritual healing. Womanists use their faith to navigate trauma, find solace, and restore a sense of wholeness. This emphasis on healing empowers womanists to confront the challenges they face with resilience and self-care.

7. Intersectional Advocacy: Religion empowers womanists to advocate for justice through an intersectional lens. It provides a framework for addressing the interconnectedness of various forms of oppression, encouraging womanists to stand up against multiple layers of discrimination.

8. Affirming Identity and Visibility: In faith spaces, womanists find opportunities for their identities to be affirmed and validated. This visibility empowers them to challenge the erasure of their experiences and to assert their rightful place within religious communities.

In essence, religion empowers womanists by providing a space for healing, resistance, and agency. By reimagining religious narratives, connecting with ancestral wisdom, and mobilizing for change, womanists harness the power of faith to confront systemic injustices and uplift their voices in pursuit of equity and liberation.

Highlight

1. Fannie Lou Hamer: Fannie Lou Hamer, a prominent civil rights activist, found strength and inspiration in her deep faith. Despite facing violent opposition and institutional racism, Hamer's unwavering faith in God fueled her determination to fight for voting rights and racial justice. She famously declared, "I'm sick and tired of being sick and tired," embodying the resilience and spiritual fortitude that guided her activism.

2. Sojourner Truth: Sojourner Truth, a former slave turned abolitionist and women's rights advocate, drew strength from her religious beliefs. Her famous "Ain't I a Woman?" speech challenged gender and racial inequalities by highlighting the inherent value bestowed upon her by her faith. Truth's unwavering conviction in the equality of all people, rooted in her faith, inspired generations of activists.

3. Ella Baker: Ella Baker, a trailblazing civil rights organizer, drew inspiration from her deeply rooted Baptist faith. Baker's commitment to grassroots organizing and empowering local communities was informed by her belief in the inherent dignity of every person. Her faith-driven dedication to fostering leadership from within communities helped shape the civil rights movement.

4. Dorothy Height: Dorothy Height, a tireless advocate for gender and racial equality, credited her faith as a guiding force in her activism. As a leader in the National Council of Negro Women, she worked to uplift the voices of Black women and foster collaboration across faith traditions. Height's faith-inspired commitment to justice laid the foundation for her impactful advocacy.

5. Septima Poinsette Clark: Septima Poinsette Clark, known as the "Queen Mother" of the Civil Rights Movement, was motivated by her Christian faith to empower African Americans through education and political participation. Her work in citizenship schools empowered countless individuals to overcome racial barriers and become active participants in democracy.

6. Bernice Johnson Reagon: Bernice Johnson Reagon, a singer, scholar, and activist, found strength in her spiritual roots as a member of the SNCC Freedom Singers during the civil rights movement. Her faith-inspired music became a powerful tool for building solidarity, fostering resilience, and lifting the spirits of those engaged in the struggle for justice.

7. Womanist Theologians: Countless womanist theologians, such as Katie Geneva Cannon, Emilie M. Townes, and Delores S. Williams, have found strength and inspiration in their faith while challenging patriarchal interpretations of religious texts. Their scholarship and activism are driven by a desire to empower marginalized communities and reshape religious narratives to align with justice and liberation.

These stories highlight the transformative power of faith in the lives of women activists. From civil rights leaders to scholars, their deep connection to their spiritual beliefs has not only fortified their personal journeys but also inspired movements for equality, justice, and social change. Through their faith, these women have exemplified the intersection of spirituality and activism, showing that strength can be found in the sacred pursuit of justice.

Spirituality, when harnessed as a force for social change, has the potential to challenge oppressive systems and inspire transformative action. It provides individuals with a framework for examining the world through a lens of justice, empathy, and interconnectedness. By leveraging their spiritual beliefs, activists can confront systemic oppression, advocate for marginalized communities, and foster a more equitable society. Here's how spirituality can be a catalyst for challenging oppressive systems:

1. Moral Imperative: Spirituality often comes with a set of ethical principles and moral imperatives. Activists can draw from these principles to challenge oppressive systems by highlighting the inherent worth and dignity of all individuals. These values provide a strong foundation for critiquing systems that perpetuate discrimination, inequality, and exploitation.

2. Empowerment and Resilience: Spirituality empowers individuals to find their inner strength and resilience. This empowerment enables activists to withstand adversity, navigate challenges, and persevere in the face of resistance from oppressive systems. Activists draw from their spiritual beliefs to fuel their determination and commitment to justice.

3. Interconnectedness and Empathy: Spirituality often emphasizes the interconnectedness of all living beings. This perspective fosters empathy and compassion for others, encouraging activists to recognize the suffering caused by oppressive systems. Activists leverage this sense of interconnectedness to advocate for systemic change that benefits all members of society.

4. Values-Driven Advocacy: Spirituality aligns with values of justice, compassion, and human dignity. Activists can frame their advocacy within a values-driven context, appealing to the shared sense of morality present in both religious and secular communities. This approach strengthens the argument against oppressive systems and galvanizes support for change.

5. Moral Accountability: Spirituality holds individuals accountable to their actions and encourages self-examination. Activists utilize this aspect of spirituality to call attention to complicity in oppressive systems, promoting personal and collective responsibility for dismantling them.

6. Community Building: Spiritual communities often serve as platforms for organizing and building solidarity. Activists tap into these communities to raise awareness about oppressive systems and mobilize collective action. Spiritual spaces provide a supportive environment for discussing systemic injustices and planning strategies for change.

7. Reclaiming Narratives: Spirituality can involve reclaiming narratives and interpreting religious teachings in ways that challenge oppressive norms. Activists reinterpret texts and traditions to support social justice efforts, undermining oppressive ideologies that may have been historically perpetuated.

8. Transformative Vision: Spirituality encourages a transformative vision for society, envisioning a world characterized by equity, compassion, and respect. Activists draw from this vision to challenge the status quo, advocating for systemic changes that align with their spiritual beliefs.

In conclusion, spirituality can be a potent tool for challenging oppressive systems by imbuing activism with values of justice, empathy, and interconnectedness. Activists who harness their spiritual beliefs drive change by appealing to shared moral imperatives, fostering resilience, building community, and reimagining a more equitable future. Through their efforts, they demonstrate that spirituality can be a driving force for dismantling oppression and promoting social transformation.

Tensions and Dilemmas

The intersection of womanist values and religious teachings often leads to complex tensions, as traditional religious norms sometimes clash with the principles of justice, equity, and empowerment central to womanism. Navigating these tensions requires a nuanced understanding of how faith and social justice intersect within the context of womanism. Let's delve into the conflicts and negotiations that arise:

1. Clashing Values: Traditional religious teachings, particularly within patriarchal interpretations, can perpetuate norms that undermine womanist principles. Concepts such as gender roles, submission, and limited agency can contradict womanist values of empowerment and autonomy. These clashes challenge womanists to critically examine and challenge oppressive interpretations.

2. Reinterpretation and Reclamation: Womanists often engage in reinterpretation and reclamation of religious texts and narratives.

They examine these sources through a lens that centers the experiences of marginalized individuals, reshaping interpretations to align with womanist principles. This process empowers womanists to reclaim their agency and challenge oppressive religious norms.

3. Intersectionality: The intersectionality of womanist identities adds another layer of complexity. For Black women, the tensions between faith and social justice are magnified by the historical context of racism and sexism. This intersection requires a sensitive negotiation of faith and values within the broader framework of social justice advocacy.

4. Challenging Hierarchies: Womanists challenge hierarchical structures within religious institutions that perpetuate discrimination and exclusion. This includes advocating for greater leadership roles for women, embracing LGBTQ+ individuals, and advocating for inclusive practices that respect diverse identities.

5. Agency and Autonomy: Womanist principles emphasize the agency and autonomy of individuals. When religious teachings restrict these aspects, tensions arise. Womanists negotiate the balance between faith and personal empowerment, often choosing interpretations that allow them to maintain their spiritual connection while asserting their autonomy.

6. Transformative Justice: Womanists advocate for transformative justice, seeking to dismantle oppressive systems. When religious teachings uphold unjust power dynamics, womanists confront the tension by advocating for interpretations that align with the pursuit of justice and equality.

7. Faith as a Source of Strength: Despite tensions, many womanists find strength and inspiration in their faith. They draw from spiritual teachings to fuel their commitment to justice, using their religious beliefs as a foundation for resistance and empowerment.

8. Embracing Complex Narratives: Negotiating tensions involves embracing the complexity of one's identity and experiences. Womanists navigate the intersections of faith, race, gender, and social justice, recognizing that their narratives are multifaceted and deserving of respect.

In essence, the clashes between womanist values and religious teachings offer opportunities for growth, transformation, and advocacy. Womanists engage in a delicate negotiation, reimagining their faith to align with principles of justice and empowerment. By challenging oppressive norms, embracing reinterpretation, and advocating for inclusive practices, womanists navigate the intricate balance between their spiritual beliefs and their commitment to social justice.

Case Studies: Womanists from Different Religious Backgrounds

1. Dr. Emilie M. Townes (Christianity): Dr. Emilie M. Townes, a womanist theologian, draws from her Christian faith to inform her activism and thought. As a scholar, she critiques traditional Christian teachings that perpetuate gender inequality and marginalization. Townes embraces womanist theology to challenge oppressive norms, using her faith as a foundation for advocating gender equity and social justice.

2. Bell Hooks (Buddhism): Bell Hooks, a feminist author and activist, practices Buddhism alongside her womanist perspectives. Her engagement with Buddhism provides her with a spiritual framework that complements her advocacy for social justice and equality. Hooks' exploration of Buddhism highlights the potential for spiritual practices to intersect with womanist principles.

3. Rev. Traci Blackmon (Christianity): Rev. Traci Blackmon, a pastor and activist, embodies the intersection of Christianity and womanism. As a leader within the United Church of Christ, she leverages her faith to challenge systemic racism, sexism, and other forms of oppression. Blackmon's activism demonstrates how religious convictions can be harnessed to effect transformative change.

4. Sikivu Hutchinson (Secular Humanism): Sikivu Hutchinson, a humanist and womanist scholar, emphasizes secular humanism in her advocacy. She explores how non-religious perspectives intersect with womanist thought, challenging the traditional narrative that faith is the only source of empowerment. Hutchinson's work highlights the complexities of reconciling womanist principles with non-theistic beliefs.

5. Raquel Evita Saraswati (Hinduism): Raquel Evita Saraswati, a womanist and Hindu scholar, navigates the intersections of Hindu spirituality and womanism. She addresses issues of caste-based discrimination, advocating for justice within her faith tradition. Saraswati's work demonstrates how womanism can influence and be influenced by diverse religious beliefs.

6. Dr. Layli Maparyan (Bahá'í Faith): Dr. Layli Maparyan, a Bahá'í scholar and womanist thinker, explores the compatibility of the Bahá'í Faith with womanist principles. Her research delves into how Bahá'í teachings intersect with social justice, emphasizing the need for gender equality and unity. Maparyan's scholarship exemplifies the complexities of navigating multiple identities.

7. LaTosha Brown (African Spirituality): LaTosha Brown, an activist and co-founder of Black Voters Matter, draws from African spirituality to inform her advocacy. She intertwines ancestral wisdom with her womanist principles, highlighting the rich heritage of spirituality within the African diaspora. Brown's work underscores the importance of cultural and spiritual connections in activism.

These case studies showcase the diverse ways in which womanists from various religious traditions navigate the complex interplay between faith, gender equity, and social justice. Each womanist demonstrates how their religious beliefs inform their activism, whether by challenging traditional norms, reimagining narratives, or emphasizing cultural heritage. Their experiences highlight the intricate journey of reconciling faith with the pursuit of equality and liberation.

Conclusion

In this chapter, we've explored the intricate relationship between faith and womanist identities, highlighting how spirituality plays a pivotal role in shaping the perspectives and activism of womanists. We've seen how faith can serve as a source of empowerment, providing strength and inspiration to challenge oppressive systems. We've examined the tensions that arise when womanist values clash with religious teachings, and how womanists negotiate these conflicts with nuanced interpretations and reclamation of narratives.

Case studies of prominent womanists from diverse religious traditions have illuminated how faith informs their activism and thought. These stories showcase the complex ways in which religious beliefs intersect with gender equity and social justice, inspiring transformative change while navigating the complexities of faith-based narratives.

As we conclude this chapter, we invite you to consider the role of your own religious background in shaping your perspectives on womanism and social justice. How does your faith influence your understanding of gender, race, and empowerment? How might your religious teachings align with or challenge womanist principles? By reflecting on these questions, you can engage more deeply with the profound relationship between faith and womanist identities, recognizing the dynamic interplay that informs the pursuit of justice, equity, and liberation.

Chapter 3: Womanist Theology: Reclaiming Spirituality for Liberation

In this chapter, we turn our attention to the enlightening realm of womanist theology and its pivotal role in the pursuit of liberation. Womanist theology stands as a dynamic response to the patriarchal interpretations that have historically dominated religious discourse. Rooted in the experiences of Black women and other marginalized individuals, womanist theology offers a transformative framework for interpreting religious texts and traditions. At its core, it embodies a commitment to justice, equity, and the holistic well-being of all.

Defining Womanist Theology: At its heart, womanist theology is a multifaceted response to the exclusionary interpretations that have often silenced the voices of women, particularly women of color, within religious contexts. It recognizes the need to counter patriarchal norms and seeks to reclaim religious narratives to reflect the diverse realities and agency of marginalized communities. In contrast to traditional interpretations, womanist theology asserts that spiritual insight can be gleaned from the experiences of those who have been historically marginalized.

Challenging Patriarchal Interpretations: Womanist theology boldly confronts patriarchal interpretations that have perpetuated harmful stereotypes and marginalized the voices of women. By critiquing these interpretations and offering alternative perspectives, womanist theology reclaims the stories of women in religious texts, fostering a deeper understanding of their roles, contributions, and agency. This reclamation serves as a vital step towards liberation.

Commitment to Justice and Equity: Central to womanist theology is an unwavering commitment to justice and equity. It recognizes that spirituality cannot be divorced from the pursuit of social justice. By intertwining the spiritual and the social, womanist theology calls for the dismantling of oppressive systems that perpetuate inequality and discrimination. It emphasizes the interconnectedness of personal liberation and societal transformation.

Holistic Well-Being: Womanist theology also emphasizes holistic well-being. It recognizes that liberation encompasses not only the external realm of systemic change but also the internal realm of emotional, spiritual, and psychological well-being. This holistic approach acknowledges that the struggle for justice is deeply intertwined with the quest for personal healing and wholeness.

As we journey through this chapter, we will delve into the foundational principles of womanist theology, exploring its transformative potential to challenge patriarchal interpretations, advocate for justice, and cultivate a deeper understanding of spirituality that resonates with the lived experiences of those who have been historically marginalized.

Emergence and Development of Womanist Theology

The emergence of womanist theology is deeply rooted in the historical context of racial and gender oppression, as well as the struggle for liberation. This context played a pivotal role in shaping the foundation and principles of womanist theology. Let's trace the historical journey that gave rise to this transformative theological framework:

1. Civil Rights and Feminist Movements: The Civil Rights Movement of the 1960s and the feminist movement of the same era laid the groundwork for womanist theology. These movements shed light on the interconnected struggles of race and gender discrimination. However, mainstream feminism often overlooked the unique challenges faced by Black women, leading to the need for a distinct theological perspective.

2. Intersectionality: The concept of intersectionality, coined by Kimberlé Crenshaw in 1989, was instrumental in shaping womanist theology. Intersectionality recognizes that individuals experience multiple forms of oppression simultaneously, and it provided a framework for understanding the unique experiences of Black women within both racial and gender contexts.

3. Alice Walker's Term "Womanist": The term "womanist" was introduced by author Alice Walker in her 1983 collection of essays titled "In Search of Our Mothers' Gardens." Walker used the term to describe Black women who were feminists but whose experiences and struggles extended beyond the feminist movement's primarily white perspective. The term "womanist" resonated with many Black women who felt excluded from both feminism and traditional religious narratives.

4. Intertwining of Race, Gender, and Spirituality: The historical experiences of Black women, marked by the legacies of slavery, colonialism, and systemic racism, compelled them to develop a theological framework that encompassed the intersections of race, gender, and spirituality. Womanist theology emerged as a response to the silencing and erasure of Black women's voices within mainstream religious discourses.

5. Reshaping Religious Narratives: As Black women scholars and activists began to engage with womanist theology, they embarked on the journey of reshaping religious narratives. They reinterpreted scripture and spiritual teachings through a womanist lens, uncovering the stories and experiences of women often overlooked by traditional interpretations.

6. Liberation and Empowerment: Womanist theology was deeply intertwined with the quest for liberation and empowerment. Black women theologians and thinkers used this framework to challenge oppressive systems, advocate for justice, and center the experiences of marginalized communities. The intersectionality of womanist theology recognized that liberation must address both racial and gender injustices.

7. Expanding Theological Discourse: The emergence of womanist theology expanded the theological discourse by introducing a perspective that validated the experiences and wisdom of Black women. It showcased the resilience, spirituality, and agency of Black women in their pursuit of liberation.

In summary, the historical context of racial and gender oppression, coupled with the exclusion of Black women from mainstream feminist and religious narratives, paved the way for the emergence of womanist theology. This theological framework rooted in intersectionality, empowerment, and liberation emerged as a transformative response to the unique experiences of Black women, shaping theology in profound and impactful ways.

Womanist theology has rich and complex roots that intertwine with liberation theology, feminist theology, and Black religious traditions. These interconnected influences have contributed to the development and distinctive nature of womanist theology, shaping its core principles and perspectives.

1. Liberation Theology: Womanist theology shares common ground with liberation theology, a movement that emerged in the mid-20th century with a focus on addressing social and political injustices. Liberation theology challenged systemic oppression and advocated for the liberation of marginalized communities. Womanist theology extends these principles to encompass the specific experiences of Black women and other marginalized groups. It draws from liberation theology's emphasis on justice, solidarity, and collective liberation while adding the lens of intersectionality.

2. Feminist Theology: Feminist theology, which emerged as a response to patriarchal interpretations of religious texts, provided a foundation for womanist theology's development. Womanist theology builds on feminist theology's critiques of gender-based oppression and exclusion. However, it expands the conversation to address the unique ways in which race intersects with gender. Womanist theology challenges the limitations of mainstream feminism, which often neglects the experiences of women of color.

3. Black Religious Traditions: Black religious traditions, deeply rooted in the history of slavery and the African diaspora, play a pivotal role in shaping womanist theology. These traditions provided a source of strength, resilience, and resistance for Black communities. Womanist theology draws inspiration from these traditions, recognizing the spiritual agency and cultural resilience that have sustained Black women through centuries of adversity. It integrates the wisdom of Black religious practices and narratives into its framework.

4. Holistic Approach: Womanist theology's roots in Black religious traditions inform its holistic approach to spirituality and justice. It acknowledges that faith is intertwined with every aspect of life, including social, political, and cultural dimensions. Womanist theology recognizes that addressing systemic oppression requires a comprehensive understanding of the interconnected nature of various forms of discrimination.

5. Collective Liberation: Influenced by both liberation theology and Black religious traditions, womanist theology emphasizes collective liberation. It recognizes that the struggle for justice must address the intersecting experiences of marginalized communities. By drawing from these roots, womanist theology seeks to dismantle oppressive systems that perpetuate inequality and advocate for the liberation of all individuals.

6. Reclamation of Narratives: Black religious traditions often involve storytelling and narratives of survival. Womanist theology embraces the reclamation of these narratives, highlighting the agency, wisdom, and resilience of Black women. This reclamation challenges patriarchal and oppressive interpretations while affirming the spiritual strength of marginalized individuals.

In essence, womanist theology emerges at the intersection of liberation theology, feminist theology, and Black religious traditions. Its unique perspective acknowledges the interconnectedness of race, gender, spirituality, and social justice. By integrating these influences, womanist theology provides a transformative framework that celebrates the agency, experiences, and narratives of Black women and other marginalized individuals within the realm of faith and theology.

The evolution of womanist theological thought over time has been marked by dynamic shifts, deepening insights, and a growing recognition of its significance within religious discourse. This evolution reflects the ongoing journey of Black women theologians and activists to articulate a theology that resonates with their lived experiences and challenges systemic injustices. Let's explore the key stages of this evolution:

1. Emergence and Articulation (1980s): The initial emergence of womanist theological thought can be traced back to the 1980s. During this period, scholars like Delores S. Williams, Jacquelyn Grant, and Katie Geneva Cannon began articulating the distinct perspectives and concerns of Black women within theological discourse. They critiqued traditional theology for its exclusionary tendencies and laid the groundwork for a theology that centered the experiences of Black women.

2. Formation of Core Principles (1990s): In the 1990s, womanist theology continued to develop its core principles. Scholars like Emilie M. Townes and Cheryl Townsend Gilkes further elaborated on the intersectionality of race, gender, and spirituality. Womanist theology began to assert itself as a transformative framework that challenged oppressive systems and promoted holistic well-being.

3. Intersectionality and Social Justice (2000s): As the concept of intersectionality gained prominence, womanist theology embraced its significance. This period saw an increased focus on the ways in which womanist theology intersects with other forms of oppression, such as class, sexuality, and ability. Womanist theologians engaged more deeply with social justice advocacy, using their theological insights to contribute to broader movements for liberation.

4. Global and Transnational Perspectives (2010s): In the 2010s, womanist theology expanded its horizons to encompass global and transnational perspectives. Scholars like Stacey Floyd-Thomas highlighted the importance of connecting womanist thought to global struggles against colonization, imperialism, and neocolonialism. Womanist theology began to engage with the experiences of women beyond the United States, recognizing the universality of their challenges.

5. Expanding Discourse (Present): In the present day, womanist theological thought continues to evolve, engaging with contemporary issues and expanding its discourse. Womanist theologians are exploring themes like environmental justice, technology, and new forms of spirituality. The ongoing evolution reflects womanist theology's adaptability and responsiveness to the changing landscape of societal challenges.

Throughout its evolution, womanist theological thought has retained its commitment to justice, equity, and the empowerment of marginalized communities. It has evolved from a response to exclusionary narratives to a vibrant and transformative framework that engages with a wide range of theological, social, and cultural issues. This evolution showcases the dynamic nature of womanist theology and its enduring relevance within the landscape of theology and social justice.

Themes of Liberation and Justice

Key Themes in Womanist Theology: Liberation, Justice, and Transformation:

- **Liberation:** Womanist theology places liberation at the forefront of its discourse. It seeks to liberate individuals and communities from the oppressive systems that perpetuate inequality, whether those systems are rooted in race, gender, class, or other forms of discrimination. Liberation involves not only dismantling external structures but also addressing internalized forms of oppression.
- **Justice:** Justice is a core theme in womanist theology, reflecting its commitment to social, political, and economic equity. Womanist theologians challenge systemic injustices and advocate for transformative change that centers marginalized voices. Justice encompasses not only legal and structural

reforms but also the restoration of dignity and agency to those who have been historically silenced.

- **Transformation:** Womanist theology envisions a transformative future where individuals, communities, and societies are reimagined and reconstructed to align with principles of equity and compassion. Transformation involves a radical shift in consciousness and values, fostering a more just and inclusive world.

Challenging Oppressive Religious Doctrines:

Womanist theology challenges oppressive religious doctrines by reinterpreting sacred texts, traditions, and teachings through a lens that centers the experiences of Black women and other marginalized individuals. It critiques patriarchal interpretations that have perpetuated harmful norms and exclusionary practices. By reclaiming narratives and promoting inclusive readings, womanist theology fosters a more accurate and empowering understanding of spirituality.

Liberation of Women, Particularly Black Women:

The liberation of women, particularly Black women, is central to womanist theological discourse. Womanist theology recognizes that the intersection of race and gender creates unique forms of oppression and marginalization. It confronts the historical erasure of Black women's experiences from religious narratives and highlights their agency, resilience, and contributions. By focusing on the liberation of Black women, womanist theology challenges the very foundations of patriarchy and racism that have shaped traditional religious teachings.

In essence, womanist theology revolves around the interconnected themes of liberation, justice, and transformation. It challenges oppressive religious doctrines by centering the experiences of marginalized individuals and promotes the liberation of women, particularly Black women, as a pivotal goal. Through these themes, womanist theology advocates for a more inclusive, equitable, and just spiritual and societal landscape.

The Intersectional Nature of Womanist Theology:

One of the defining features of womanist theology is its intersectional nature. Womanist theologians recognize that individuals hold multiple identities that interact and intersect to shape their experiences. This intersectionality extends beyond race and gender to include factors like class, sexuality, ability, and more. This holistic approach allows womanist theology to address the complexities of individuals' lives and the various forms of oppression they may face.

Addressing Intersectionality:

Womanist theologians tackle the intersections of race, gender, class, and sexuality by acknowledging the ways these identities interact to shape individuals' realities. They critique approaches that view oppression as separate and compartmentalized, recognizing that various forms of discrimination are interconnected. For instance, a Black woman's experience is not solely defined by her race or her gender; it's the intricate interplay of both, as well as other factors, that shapes her life.

Role of Lived Experiences:

Lived experiences play a pivotal role in shaping womanist theological perspectives. Womanist theologians emphasize the importance of listening to and valuing the stories of individuals who have been marginalized. These narratives provide insights into the effects of systemic injustices and inform theological reflections. By centering lived experiences, womanist theology grounds its principles in the realities of those most affected by oppression.

Examples of Intersectional Approach:

- **Race and Gender:** Womanist theologians critique racial and gender biases within religious texts and traditions. They analyze how Black women have been marginalized in theological narratives, leading to the development of alternative interpretations that uplift the stories of previously silenced figures.
- **Class and Socioeconomic Status:** Womanist theology addresses the economic disparities that affect marginalized

communities, especially Black women. It critiques the prosperity gospel and challenges the notion that material wealth equates to spiritual favor.

- **Sexuality and Identity:** Womanist theologians consider the intersections of sexuality and gender identity within Black women's experiences. They challenge heteronormative assumptions within religious spaces and advocate for LGBTQ+ inclusivity.
- **Ability and Disability:** Womanist theology engages with issues of ableism and disability, recognizing the impact of physical and mental disabilities on individuals' lives. It advocates for accessibility and dismantles notions of worth based on ability.

In conclusion, the intersectional nature of womanist theology acknowledges the multifaceted identities of individuals and addresses the interconnected forms of oppression they face. Womanist theologians listen to lived experiences, challenge traditional narratives, and embrace an inclusive approach that reflects the complexity of human existence. Through this lens, womanist theology fosters a more inclusive, compassionate, and justice-centered understanding of spirituality and social engagement.

The Power of Storytelling and Narrative

The Significance of Storytelling in Womanist Theology:

Storytelling holds a profound significance within womanist theology, as it serves as a powerful tool for preserving history, wisdom, and lived experiences. Storytelling is not merely a means of communication; it is a way of sharing knowledge, affirming identity, and challenging oppressive narratives. In womanist theology, storytelling reclaims the narratives of marginalized communities, particularly Black women, and offers an alternative perspective that centers their voices and experiences.

The Importance of Narrative and Oral Traditions:

Narratives and oral traditions play a crucial role in preserving history and wisdom, especially when marginalized voices have been excluded from written records. In many cultures, oral traditions are the primary means of passing down knowledge from one generation to another. These traditions are a way of connecting with ancestral wisdom, acknowledging the past, and transmitting values and lessons that inform the present and future.

Challenging Dominant Religious Narratives:

Womanist narratives challenge dominant religious narratives by offering alternative perspectives that disrupt established norms. Traditional religious narratives often marginalize or silence the experiences of Black women and other marginalized groups. Womanist stories reclaim these narratives, providing a space for individuals to see themselves reflected in the divine and spiritual landscape. These narratives also challenge oppressive interpretations by highlighting the agency, resilience, and contributions of those who have been historically sidelined.

Examples of Womanist Narratives:

- **Reimagining Biblical Stories:** Womanist narratives reinterpret biblical stories to center the experiences of women, particularly women of color. They offer fresh insights into characters and events often overshadowed by patriarchal interpretations.
- **Ancestral Wisdom:** Womanist narratives draw from ancestral wisdom and oral traditions, acknowledging the importance of interconnectedness with the past. These narratives celebrate cultural resilience and pass down knowledge that is often excluded from mainstream historical accounts.
- **Personal Testimonies:** Womanist narratives often incorporate personal testimonies and experiences, allowing individuals to share their own stories of triumph, struggle, and spiritual growth. These narratives create a space for individuals to voice their truths and affirm their identities.
- **Community Narratives:** Womanist narratives highlight the significance of community stories, amplifying the collective wisdom and shared experiences of marginalized communities.

They offer a counter-narrative to individualistic perspectives that often dominate religious discourse.

In essence, storytelling in womanist theology is a potent means of challenging dominant narratives, preserving history, and affirming identity. It enables marginalized voices to be heard, their experiences to be acknowledged, and their wisdom to be shared. Through these narratives, womanist theology engages in a transformative process that reshapes the spiritual landscape by centering the stories of those who have been historically excluded.

Womanist Theology in Practice

Examples of Womanist Theological Writings and Analyses:

- **Delores S. Williams' "Sisters in the Wilderness":** In this seminal work, Williams explores womanist theology through the lens of Hagar's story in the Bible. She critiques traditional interpretations that have overlooked the struggles of Black women and examines how Hagar's narrative resonates with the experiences of marginalized women.
- **Jacquelyn Grant's "White Women's Christ and Black Women's Jesus":** Grant critically examines traditional depictions of Christ and challenges their Eurocentric and patriarchal biases. She offers a womanist perspective that centers the experiences and needs of Black women within the Christian tradition.
- **Kelly Brown Douglas' "Stand Your Ground: Black Bodies and the Justice of God":** Douglas addresses the intersection of racism and gender violence within Christianity. She analyzes the "stand your ground" culture and explores the role of religion in the pursuit of justice for Black lives.

Informing Activism, Advocacy, and Social Change:

Womanist theology deeply informs activism, advocacy, and social change by providing a theological framework that centers justice, liberation, and holistic well-being. Womanist theologians draw insights from their spiritual beliefs to fuel their commitment to transformative action:

- **Liberation Theology:** Womanist theology's emphasis on liberation and justice directly informs activism aimed at dismantling oppressive systems. It motivates individuals to challenge structures of inequality and work towards a more just society.
- **Intersectional Advocacy:** Womanist theology's recognition of intersectionality guides advocacy efforts that address multiple forms of oppression. It encourages individuals to understand the interconnectedness of issues and engage in advocacy that respects the diverse experiences of marginalized communities.
- **Empowerment:** Womanist theology empowers individuals to recognize their agency and resilience, motivating them to engage in advocacy that uplifts their communities. It encourages people to see themselves as agents of change rather than passive recipients of oppression.

Practical Implications of Womanist Theological Principles:

- **Inclusive Worship:** Womanist theology challenges religious institutions to create worship spaces that are inclusive of diverse identities, experiences, and cultural practices. This involves reimagining rituals, liturgy, and symbolism to reflect the richness of marginalized communities.
- **Community Empowerment:** Womanist theology encourages community-based initiatives that address social and economic disparities. It emphasizes the importance of building strong, supportive networks that promote holistic well-being.
- **Educational Equity:** Womanist theological principles advocate for educational systems that prioritize the voices and histories of marginalized communities. This involves curriculum changes that accurately reflect the contributions of Black women and other historically silenced groups.
- **Cultural Preservation:** Womanist theology emphasizes the importance of preserving cultural traditions, oral histories, and ancestral wisdom. This has practical implications for cultural preservation initiatives and the transmission of knowledge across generations.

In summary, womanist theological writings and analyses offer profound insights into the experiences of marginalized communities.

These insights inform activism, advocacy, and social change by providing a theological foundation for justice and liberation. The practical implications of womanist theological principles guide efforts to create inclusive worship spaces, empower communities, promote educational equity, and preserve cultural heritage.

Addressing Criticisms and Challenges:

Womanist theology, like any theological framework, has faced criticisms and challenges. Some critiques include:

- **Exclusivity:** Critics argue that womanist theology focuses primarily on the experiences of Black women and may exclude the voices of other marginalized groups.
- **Marginalization of LGBTQ+ Voices:** Some critics highlight that womanist theology hasn't consistently addressed LGBTQ+ issues, leading to concerns about inclusivity within its discourse.
- **Integration with Traditional Theology:** Some question the compatibility of womanist theology with traditional religious doctrines, particularly in more conservative religious contexts.
- **Religious Pluralism:** Critics argue that womanist theology doesn't always accommodate the diverse religious beliefs within Black communities, potentially excluding those who don't adhere to Christian traditions.

Debates and Traditional Religious Institutions:

Debates within womanist theology often revolve around its relationship with traditional religious institutions:

- **Orthodoxy and Innovation:** Some womanist theologians seek to reform traditional religious structures from within, while others advocate for more radical transformations that challenge established norms.
- **Gender and Leadership:** Womanist theology raises questions about gender roles and leadership within religious institutions, spurring discussions about inclusivity and equity in roles like clergy and religious leadership.
- **Doctrine and Practice:** Debates arise regarding how womanist theology navigates traditional religious doctrines. Some theologians reinterpret scriptures, while others critique the very foundations of these doctrines.

Ongoing Dialogue within Womanist Thought:

Womanist thought is characterized by its dynamic nature and ongoing dialogue:

- **Intersectional Expansions:** Womanist theologians continue to expand intersectionality to include dimensions like ability, immigration status, and more, recognizing the evolving complexity of identities.
- **Global Perspectives:** Womanist theology increasingly engages with global and transnational issues, acknowledging the interconnectedness of struggles across diverse contexts.
- **Inclusivity Efforts:** Womanist theology actively works to address critiques of exclusivity and foster a more inclusive dialogue that acknowledges the diverse experiences of all marginalized groups.
- **Interfaith Exploration:** Some womanist theologians explore the intersection of womanist thought with other faith traditions, contributing to interfaith dialogue and understanding.

In conclusion, womanist theology faces criticisms related to inclusivity, LGBTQ+ issues, compatibility with traditional theology, and religious pluralism. Debates within womanist theology often center on its relationship with traditional religious institutions, ranging from reforms to radical transformation. The ongoing dialogue within womanist thought reflects its commitment to intersectional expansion, global perspectives, inclusivity efforts, and interfaith exploration.

Chapter Summary:

In this chapter, we've delved into the captivating realm of womanist theology—a transformative framework that centers the experiences of Black women and other marginalized groups within religious discourse. We explored how womanist theology emerges at the crossroads of liberation, justice, and transformation, challenging oppressive religious doctrines and advocating for the holistic well-being of individuals and communities.

Transformative Potential for Both Religious and Secular Spaces:

Womanist theology holds immense transformative potential, not only within religious spaces but also in the secular realm. By centering justice, equity, and liberation, womanist theological perspectives challenge systemic inequalities and inspire activism, advocacy, and social change. The principles of womanist theology can inform a more inclusive understanding of spirituality, social engagement, and personal empowerment.

Engaging with Womanist Theological Perspectives:

We encourage you, the reader, to engage thoughtfully with womanist theological perspectives. Consider the ways in which womanist theology offers a dynamic response to patriarchal interpretations, intersectional challenges, and the historical silencing of marginalized voices. Explore how narratives and oral traditions weave together histories, wisdom, and resistance. Reflect on the significance of womanist theological principles in shaping both personal and collective narratives of liberation and justice.

Implications for Liberation and Justice:

By embracing womanist theological perspectives, you embark on a journey that dismantles oppressive structures and fosters a deeper connection between faith, social justice, and personal identity. As you delve into the intricate relationship between faith and womanist identities, recognize the power of intersectionality in feminist discourse and the potential of womanist theology to challenge and transform both religious and secular spaces.

As you move forward, we invite you to engage with womanist theology not as a mere academic pursuit, but as a call to action—a call to envision a world where justice, equity, and liberation are not just ideals, but lived realities. Let the wisdom of womanist theology inspire you to contribute to the ongoing dialogue for a more just and inclusive society.

Chapter 4: Beneath Patriarchal Shadows: How Religion Has Subjugated Women

Introduction to the Chapter's Exploration: Ways Religion Historically Subjugated Women:

In this chapter, we embark on a journey to uncover a complex and often unsettling history—how religion has historically played a role in the subjugation of women. Throughout the ages, religious institutions have held immense influence over societies, shaping beliefs, norms, and values. Within this intricate tapestry, we'll unravel the threads that reveal the ways in which women have been marginalized, silenced, and oppressed within the realm of religious teachings and practices.

Pervasive Influence of Patriarchal Structures within Religious Institutions:

Central to our exploration is the recognition of patriarchal structures that have permeated religious institutions. These structures have perpetuated power imbalances and upheld gender norms that limit the agency and autonomy of women. Within this context, we'll delve into how religious texts, interpretations, and leadership roles have often reinforced a narrative that relegates women to subservient roles, constraining their potential for spiritual, social, and personal growth.

The Importance of Acknowledging and Understanding Historical Context:

As we navigate this examination, it is crucial to underscore the significance of acknowledging and understanding historical context. The societal norms and power dynamics that existed in the past have greatly influenced religious beliefs and practices. By comprehending the historical context in which religious texts were written and interpreted, we gain insight into how women's identities were constructed and, at times, suppressed.

By venturing into this chapter, we confront a challenging aspect of history—one that calls for critical reflection, compassion, and a commitment to dismantling harmful narratives. Our exploration aims not only to shed light on the past but also to catalyze conversations about the role of religion in shaping gender dynamics and to inspire a collective movement towards a more equitable and inclusive future.

Historical Context of Patriarchy and Religion

Tracing the Roots of Patriarchal Religious Structures in Ancient Societies:

To understand the origins of patriarchal religious structures, we must journey back through time to ancient societies where the foundations of gender norms and power dynamics were laid. In these early civilizations, religious beliefs and practices were intertwined with social structures, shaping the roles and statuses assigned to men and women.

1. Ancient Mesopotamia: In Mesopotamia, one of the world's earliest civilizations, religious institutions were closely tied to the ruling elite. Goddesses were venerated as symbols of fertility and life, but as power shifted toward a more hierarchical society, male deities assumed more dominant roles. Temples and religious positions became controlled by male priests, establishing a pattern of male authority.

2. Ancient Egypt: In ancient Egypt, religion played a central role in both public and private life. Although women had more legal rights and participation in religious practices compared to other societies, the highest religious positions were predominantly held by men. The pharaoh, who often held religious significance, was traditionally male.

3. Ancient Greece and Rome: Greek and Roman societies featured patriarchal religious structures where gods and goddesses mirrored societal hierarchies. Despite the veneration of goddesses, religious leadership roles were reserved for men. Women were often relegated to secondary roles and were subject to male authority.

4. Ancient Abrahamic Traditions: The Abrahamic religions—Judaism, Christianity, and Islam—emerged in patriarchal societies. While these traditions contain diverse narratives about women, interpretations have historically leaned toward reinforcing gender norms. In some cases, religious texts were interpreted to justify women's subordination and limited participation in religious leadership.

5. Mythology and Creation Narratives: Mythology from various cultures often portrayed male deities as creators and rulers, contributing to the normalization of patriarchal norms. Creation narratives often depicted women as created from or for men, reinforcing notions of male dominance.

The roots of patriarchal religious structures lie in the confluence of social, cultural, and religious factors within ancient societies. These structures mirrored and perpetuated broader gender hierarchies that had societal implications beyond religious contexts. While these historical foundations set the stage, it's important to note that resistance, reinterpretation, and change have also been part of the ongoing dialogue surrounding gender dynamics within religious frameworks.

Impact of Religious Texts and Narratives on Gender Norms:

Religious texts and narratives have exerted profound influence on shaping and reinforcing gender norms throughout history. These texts are not only sources of spiritual guidance but also repositories of cultural values and societal expectations. The interpretations and teachings derived from religious texts have played a significant role in establishing and perpetuating traditional gender roles, often to the detriment of women's status and agency.

1. Reinforcement of Traditional Roles: Religious narratives have frequently depicted women in roles that align with traditional gender norms. Stories of obedient wives, nurturing mothers, and virtuous daughters have been highlighted, often reinforcing the expectation that women's primary roles revolve around caregiving and subservience to men.

2. Theology of Submission: Certain interpretations of religious texts have been used to promote a theology of submission, suggesting that women should defer to male authority in both religious and societal matters. This theological framework has been employed to justify unequal power dynamics within marriages, leadership roles, and decision-making processes.

3. Reproduction of Patriarchal Ideals: Religious texts have sometimes been used to legitimize and reproduce patriarchal ideals. For instance, biblical accounts such as Eve's creation from Adam's rib have been interpreted to establish a hierarchical order in which men are seen as superior and women as secondary.

4. Silence and Erasure: The absence or marginalization of women's voices within religious narratives has contributed to their erasure from historical and theological discourse. Women's perspectives, experiences, and contributions have often been minimized or left unrecorded, reinforcing the notion that their presence is of lesser importance.

5. Challenging and Reinterpreting Texts: Despite these pervasive patterns, religious texts also contain narratives that challenge gender norms. Certain figures, such as prophetesses, queens, and strong female characters, offer alternative models of leadership and agency. Some scholars and communities have engaged in reinterpretations that challenge traditional readings, emphasizing themes of equality, justice, and liberation.

6. Potential for Change: It's important to recognize that religious texts are not monolithic; they encompass diverse stories and teachings that can be interpreted in multiple ways. Many individuals and communities are working to reclaim and reinterpret these texts, using them as sources of inspiration for advocating gender equality, social justice, and empowerment.

In summary, religious texts and narratives have deeply influenced gender norms by both reinforcing traditional roles and providing potential for reimagining them. Interpretations have played a significant role in shaping societal expectations, but they also offer space for dialogue, change, and the exploration of alternative narratives that challenge and transform prevailing gender norms.

Examining Historical Examples of Women's Limited Roles within Religious Contexts:

Throughout history, women's roles within religious contexts have often been constrained by societal norms and interpretations of religious teachings. While there are exceptions, many examples highlight the challenges and limitations that women have faced in their engagement with religious institutions and practices:

1. Ancient Priesthoods: In various ancient civilizations, priesthoods were typically reserved for men. Women had limited access to religious leadership roles and were often excluded from officiating rituals or holding positions of authority within religious hierarchies.

2. Early Christianity: In early Christian communities, women's participation was encouraged but often confined to supportive roles. The apostolic tradition and interpretations of biblical passages led to restrictions on women's ordination and leadership within formal religious structures.

3. Islamic Traditions: Islamic history features a complex range of interpretations regarding women's roles. While women contributed significantly to the early Islamic community, cultural practices and interpretations of religious texts have led to varying levels of gender segregation and limited access to certain religious spaces.

4. Hinduism and Caste Systems: In traditional Hindu societies, women's roles have been deeply intertwined with caste systems and patriarchal norms. While goddess worship exists, women's spiritual authority has often been overshadowed by the male-centered priestly class.

5. Judaism and Synagogue Participation: In Judaism, women's roles within synagogues were traditionally limited. While they participated in various rituals, they were often separated from men and excluded from certain leadership and liturgical roles.

6. Buddhist Monasticism: Within some Buddhist traditions, women have historically faced barriers to full ordination and participation in monastic life. Gender-based restrictions have limited their access to higher levels of spiritual practice and leadership.

7. Indigenous Spiritual Traditions: In many indigenous spiritual traditions, women's roles have been both significant and complex. However, colonial influences and missionary efforts often disrupted traditional practices, sometimes leading to the erasure of women's spiritual leadership.

8. Witch Hunts and Persecution: During periods of history marked by witch hunts and persecution, women who exhibited unconventional spiritual practices were often targeted. Accusations of witchcraft and heresy curtailed women's autonomy and spiritual expression.

While these historical examples showcase women's limited roles within religious contexts, it's important to note that women have also been agents of change, pushing boundaries and advocating for expanded roles. As societies evolve and reinterpret religious teachings, there has been a growing recognition of the need to challenge and transform these historical limitations to create more inclusive and equitable religious spaces.

Religious Justifications for Women's Subjugation

Analyzing Religious Interpretations Perpetuating Women's Subjugation:

Throughout history, certain religious interpretations have contributed to the subjugation of women, reinforcing unequal gender dynamics. These interpretations have often been shaped by patriarchal norms and societal expectations, leading to the marginalization, silencing, and restriction of women's agency. Here are some key ways in which religious interpretations have perpetuated women's subjugation:

1. Textual Literalism: Interpreting religious texts literally without considering historical context or metaphorical elements has led to the reinforcement of patriarchal norms. Verses that appear to endorse male authority and female submission have been taken at face value, sidelining broader messages of equality and justice.

2. Eve's Blame in Abrahamic Traditions: Interpreting stories like the Fall of Adam and Eve in Abrahamic traditions has often placed blame on Eve, portraying her as responsible for humanity's expulsion from paradise. This interpretation has been used to justify women's subservient roles as punishment for Eve's actions.

3. Veiling and Modesty: Interpretations of religious texts within Islam, Christianity, and other traditions have led to the imposition of strict dress codes and veiling for women. These interpretations link women's piety and virtue to their modesty, reinforcing the idea that their worth lies in their physical appearance and adherence to male-defined standards.

4. Leadership Restrictions: Interpretations of religious texts have been used to justify restrictions on women's leadership roles within religious institutions. Some passages have been cited to exclude women from priesthoods, clerical roles, and decision-making positions, reinforcing the notion that religious leadership is reserved for men.

5. Body and Purity: Interpretations of religious purity laws have often centered around women's bodies. Menstrual taboos, for example, have been interpreted as implying women's impurity, leading to exclusion from religious rituals and spaces during menstruation.

6. Concepts of Obedience and Submission: Some interpretations emphasize concepts of women's obedience and submission to male authority, within both religious and marital contexts. These interpretations can lead to the justification of controlling behaviors and limit women's autonomy.

7. Limited Access to Knowledge: Interpretations that restrict women's access to religious education and scholarship have perpetuated their marginalization. By denying women the opportunity to engage with theological debates and texts, these interpretations reinforce unequal power dynamics.

8. Erasure of Women's Contributions: Selective interpretations that overlook or dismiss women's contributions to religious history and theology contribute to their erasure from the narrative. This reinforces the perception that women's voices and perspectives are secondary or inconsequential.

It's important to emphasize that interpretations are not fixed; they can evolve and be reexamined. Many contemporary scholars and communities are engaging in reinterpretation efforts to challenge these harmful narratives and highlight more egalitarian and inclusive readings of religious texts. This ongoing dialogue is vital in creating spaces where religious interpretations promote justice, equality, and the empowerment of all individuals, regardless of gender.

Scriptures and Teachings Used to Justify Gender Hierarchy:

Throughout history, specific scriptures and teachings from various religious traditions have been selectively interpreted and used to justify gender hierarchy, reinforcing unequal power dynamics between men and women. These interpretations often reflect societal norms and patriarchal values, perpetuating women's subordination and limiting their roles. Here are some notable examples:

1. Biblical Subordination: Within Christianity, certain passages from the Bible have been cited to justify the idea of women's subordination to men. Ephesians 5:22-24, for instance, has been interpreted to command wives to submit to their husbands. Such passages have been used to legitimize hierarchical marriage dynamics and limit women's agency.

2. Head Coverings in Christianity and Islam: In both Christianity and Islam, teachings about modesty and head coverings have been interpreted in ways that emphasize women's submission to male authority. For instance, 1 Corinthians 11:3-10 in the New Testament and various interpretations of hijab in Islam have been used to symbolize women's modesty and their need to cover their bodies for the sake of male "protection" or "honor."

3. Gender Roles in Hinduism: In some interpretations of Hinduism, scriptures like Manusmriti have been cited to emphasize gender roles and duties. These interpretations assign specific responsibilities to men and women, reinforcing traditional family structures and notions of obedience.

4. Leadership Exclusion in Many Traditions: Religious teachings have often been used to justify the exclusion of women from leadership roles. Some interpretations cite the male apostles' leadership in Christianity, the exclusion of women from priesthood in various traditions, and the historical absence of female prophets or religious leaders as evidence of a divine intention for male leadership.

5. Reinterpretation as Intrinsic Hierarchy: In some interpretations, the creation story itself has been used to justify a hierarchical relationship between genders. The creation of Eve from Adam's rib has been interpreted to symbolize her secondary status, suggesting that women are meant to be subservient to men.

6. Limited Ritual Participation: Interpretations that restrict women's participation in certain religious rituals have been used to reinforce gender hierarchy. Women's exclusion from rituals or roles in temples, synagogues, and mosques has been justified by interpreting historical practices as reflective of inherent gender differences.

It's crucial to acknowledge that these interpretations are not universally accepted within religious communities. Many scholars and believers engage in critical analysis and reinterpretation to challenge these perspectives and promote more inclusive, equitable readings of sacred texts. The ways in which religious teachings have been interpreted to justify gender hierarchy highlight the need for ongoing dialogue and thoughtful engagement with scriptures to ensure that interpretations reflect justice, equality, and the inherent dignity of all individuals.

Role of Religious Leaders in Reinforcing Patriarchal Norms:

Religious leaders have historically played a significant role in reinforcing patriarchal norms within religious communities and society at large. Their influence on interpretation, practice, and communal dynamics has contributed to the perpetuation of unequal gender dynamics. Here's how religious leaders have reinforced patriarchal norms:

1. Interpretation and Teaching: Religious leaders often hold authority in interpreting sacred texts and teachings. When interpretations prioritize patriarchal readings, these leaders reinforce gender norms that position men as leaders and women as followers. Their teachings can shape perceptions of gender roles and relationships.

2. Sermons and Discourses: In sermons and religious discourses, leaders have occasionally emphasized traditional gender roles, presenting women as virtuous when fulfilling submissive roles and men as leaders in religious and societal matters. These messages reinforce societal expectations and discourage questioning of established norms.

3. Leadership Structures: Many religious institutions have been historically led by men, and this leadership imbalance has been perpetuated by religious leaders themselves. Male clergy and religious leaders occupying higher positions have conveyed a visual representation of male authority, reinforcing the idea of gender hierarchy.

4. Silence on Gender Equality: When religious leaders remain silent on issues of gender equality or fail to address the negative impact of patriarchal norms, they implicitly endorse the status quo. Their failure to advocate for justice and gender equity can perpetuate harmful ideologies.

5. Exclusion of Women from Leadership: Religious leaders who support or enforce policies that exclude women from leadership roles further reinforce patriarchal norms. This exclusion sends a clear message about the perceived limitations of women's capabilities and contributions.

6. Policing Women's Behavior: In some instances, religious leaders have acted as enforcers of gender norms, scrutinizing and policing women's behavior and attire. This surveillance further reinforces patriarchal norms that prioritize male-defined standards of modesty and virtue.

7. Discrediting Feminist Voices: In response to challenges to patriarchal norms, religious leaders have at times discredited feminist voices by labeling them as anti-religious or heretical. This marginalization discourages open dialogue about gender equity within religious spaces.

8. Justification of Gender-Based Violence: In extreme cases, religious leaders have used interpretations of religious texts to justify or downplay gender-based violence. By framing abuse as a consequence of women's failure to adhere to their prescribed roles, these leaders enable harm.

While it's essential to acknowledge that not all religious leaders perpetuate patriarchal norms, those who do hold significant influence over shaping communal attitudes and perceptions. Religious leaders who recognize the potential for positive change can play a pivotal role in challenging and transforming patriarchal norms within religious communities. By promoting inclusive interpretations, advocating for gender equity, and engaging in respectful dialogue, religious leaders can contribute to fostering more just and equitable religious spaces.

Impact on Women's Social Roles and Agency

Examining How Religious Teachings Have Shaped Women's Societal Roles:

Religious teachings have played a significant role in shaping societal roles for women by influencing cultural norms, expectations, and behaviors. These teachings, often interpreted through patriarchal lenses, have contributed to defining women's place within families, communities, and broader society. Here's how religious teachings have impacted women's societal roles:

1. Family and Marriage Roles: Religious teachings have often emphasized women's roles as wives, mothers, and caretakers. Narratives highlighting virtues like submission and self-sacrifice have reinforced the idea that women's primary purpose lies in domestic and caregiving responsibilities.

2. Modesty and Purity Ideals: Religious teachings about modesty and purity have shaped how women's bodies and behaviors are perceived. Concepts of covering and modest dressing have been interpreted as upholding women's honor and virtue, reinforcing the notion that their worth is tied to their appearance.

3. Restrictions on Economic Activity: Some religious teachings have limited women's engagement in economic activities outside the home, prioritizing their roles as homemakers. This has contributed to gendered divisions of labor and financial dependency.

4. Education and Intellectual Pursuits: Certain interpretations of religious teachings have limited women's access to education and intellectual pursuits. The emphasis on women's roles within the home has historically been used to justify restricting their opportunities for formal education.

5. Leadership and Decision-Making: Religious teachings have been used to justify limited women's participation in leadership and decision-making roles within religious and societal contexts. The lack of female religious leaders and exclusion from decision-making processes perpetuates gender inequality.

6. Limited Roles in Religious Institutions: In many religious traditions, women's roles within religious institutions have been restricted. They have often been excluded from positions of religious authority, preventing them from participating fully in the interpretation of sacred texts and the guidance of their communities.

7. Spiritual Authority and Rituals: Certain religious teachings have withheld spiritual authority and participation in rituals from women. This exclusion from rituals and religious leadership has contributed to a perception of women as spiritually subordinate.

8. Policing of Behavior and Morality: Religious teachings that prescribe strict codes of behavior and morality have disproportionately affected women. These teachings have been used to enforce norms around sexuality, modesty, and social interactions, often placing the burden of moral purity on women.

9. Silence and Marginalization: Interpretations of religious texts that silence or marginalize women's voices have contributed to their invisibility within religious narratives. This lack of representation reinforces the perception that women's perspectives are less significant.

In conclusion, religious teachings have historically played a central role in shaping women's societal roles. While these teachings have often reinforced patriarchal norms and limitations, it's important to recognize that interpretations are not static. Many individuals and communities are actively engaging in reinterpretation efforts to challenge and transform these restrictive narratives, advocating for more inclusive, equitable, and empowering interpretations of religious teachings.

Instances of Women Challenging Patriarchal Religious Norms:

Throughout history, courageous women have risen against patriarchal religious norms, advocating for equality, justice, and expanded roles within religious contexts. Their stories stand as beacons of resistance and change:

1. Historical Figures: Women like Hildegard of Bingen in Christianity, Rabia Basri in Islam, and Mirabai in Hinduism challenged conventional norms by engaging in theological discourse, composing hymns, and expressing their spirituality on their terms.

2. Suffragettes and Women's Movements: In the late 19th and early 20th centuries, suffragettes and women's rights activists drew inspiration from religious teachings to demand political and social equality. They highlighted shared values of justice and human dignity found in religious texts.

3. Feminist Theologians: Feminist theologians, such as Mary Daly and Rosemary Radford Ruether, critiqued patriarchal interpretations of religious texts. They sought to reinterpret scripture in ways that empower women and challenge oppressive norms.

4. Liberation Theology: Liberation theology movements, originating in contexts of social injustice and inequality, have often emphasized the inherent worth and dignity of all individuals. Some variations have explicitly advocated for gender equality and women's rights.

5. Intersectional Activism: Contemporary intersectional feminist movements incorporate spirituality into their activism. Black feminist activists, for example, have drawn upon their religious backgrounds to challenge racism, sexism, and other forms of oppression.

6. Indigenous Resistance: Indigenous women worldwide have defended their spiritual practices and challenged attempts to suppress their cultural and religious identities, demonstrating resilience against patriarchal colonial influences.

7. Progressive Religious Communities: Within various religious traditions, progressive movements have emerged that challenge traditional interpretations and advocate for gender equity and LGBTQ+ inclusion, demonstrating that religious teachings can be vehicles for change.

Religious and Secular Movements for Women's Rights:

Religious and secular movements for women's rights have converged to challenge patriarchal structures and advocate for equality:

1. Women's Suffrage Movement: The women's suffrage movement sought political equality for women, drawing on principles of justice and human rights that are often rooted in religious teachings.

2. International Women's Day: International Women's Day celebrates the achievements and contributions of women while highlighting ongoing gender inequalities. It is a platform for women across cultures, faiths, and backgrounds to come together in solidarity.

3. Women's Empowerment in Islam: In recent years, Muslim women have been engaged in discussions about interpretations of Islamic teachings. They have advocated for more inclusive understandings that promote gender equality and justice.

4. Religious Feminism: Religious feminists bridge their faith with feminist principles, challenging patriarchal interpretations and advocating for women's expanded roles in religious leadership, rituals, and decision-making.

Role of Womanism and Feminist Theology:

1. Womanism: Rooted in Black feminism, womanism emphasizes the intersectionality of race, gender, and class. Womanist theology critiques patriarchal structures, advocating for the voices and experiences of Black women and other marginalized groups.

2. Feminist Theology: Feminist theology deconstructs patriarchal interpretations of religious texts, revealing hidden biases and empowering women to reclaim their spiritual agency and explore divine femininity.

3. Liberation Theology: Liberation theology, influenced by feminist perspectives, examines how systems of oppression intersect. It addresses social injustice through the lens of faith, advocating for marginalized communities' liberation.

4. Interfaith Activism: Interfaith activism brings together women from diverse religious backgrounds to challenge patriarchal norms that exist across faiths. This collaboration amplifies the collective voice against gender inequality.

In conclusion, the history of women challenging patriarchal religious norms is rich and diverse. From historical figures to contemporary movements, women have consistently defied limitations to reshape religious spaces and advocate for justice. Religious and secular movements for women's rights continue to work in tandem, creating a more inclusive and equitable world where all individuals can fully exercise their agency and dignity.

Intersections of Race and Gender Oppression:

The intersections of race and gender oppression create unique and complex challenges, particularly for women of color. These compounded forms of discrimination can lead to overlapping and interlocking systems of marginalization, limiting opportunities and shaping experiences. Understanding these intersections is essential for addressing the multifaceted nature of oppression:

1. Compounded Impact on Women of Color: Women of color often face a compounded impact of racism and sexism. Their experiences are shaped not only by gender-based inequalities but also by racial disparities, leading to specific challenges and barriers that differ from those faced by white women or men of color.

2. Multiple Marginalizations: The concept of intersectionality recognizes that women of color may experience multiple forms of marginalization beyond race and gender, such as socioeconomic status, sexual orientation, and disability. These intersecting identities contribute to their unique lived experiences.

3. Cultural Erasure and Stereotyping: Women of color frequently confront cultural erasure, where their identities are overlooked or misrepresented. Stereotyping based on both race and gender can perpetuate harmful narratives and limit their agency.

4. Representation and Leadership: In various sectors, including religious contexts, women of color often face limited representation and leadership opportunities. The lack of diverse role models can reinforce the perception that their voices and experiences are less valuable.

Racialized Misogyny within Religious Contexts:

Within religious contexts, racialized misogyny operates as a unique form of discrimination that targets women of color. This form of oppression is characterized by the intersection of racial prejudice and gender bias, leading to specific challenges:

1. Stereotyping and Hypersexualization: Racialized misogyny can involve the hypersexualization of women of color, perpetuating harmful stereotypes that objectify and demean them. This often leads to the fetishization of their bodies and identities.

2. Religious Colonialism: In the context of colonial history, women of color have endured the effects of religious institutions that imposed patriarchal norms alongside racial hierarchies. This has contributed to the erasure of indigenous spiritual practices and identities.

3. Cultural Appropriation and Exoticism: Some religious practices have been appropriated and commodified, further marginalizing women of color. Their cultural and spiritual practices are often exploited for aesthetic purposes, reinforcing racial and gender stereotypes.

Womanist Responses to Intersectional Oppression:

1. Intersectional Advocacy: Womanism, with its focus on intersectionality, provides a framework for addressing the interconnectedness of race and gender oppression. It encourages a holistic understanding of identity that uplifts the experiences of women of color.

2. Empowerment and Solidarity: Womanism fosters empowerment and solidarity among women of color by acknowledging their shared experiences and advocating for their liberation. It emphasizes the importance of centering their voices and perspectives.

3. Challenging Religious Structures: Womanist theology challenges patriarchal and racist interpretations of religious texts and practices. It calls for a more inclusive and just understanding of spirituality that honors the complexities of women of color's identities.

4. Resisting Erasure: Womanism seeks to resist the erasure of women of color's contributions to religious traditions. It highlights the importance of recognizing and reclaiming their spiritual heritage.

In essence, understanding the intersections of race and gender oppression is crucial for dismantling systemic inequalities within religious spaces and beyond. Womanism offers a powerful framework for addressing these complex issues, advocating for the liberation and empowerment of women of color in both spiritual and secular realms.

Unearthing Hidden Narratives: Lesser-Known Stories of Women's Resistance and Leadership:

Throughout history, there exists a tapestry of lesser-known narratives that highlight women's remarkable acts of resistance, leadership, and defiance against patriarchal religious norms. These stories, often overshadowed by dominant historical narratives, unveil the strength and courage of women who challenged the status quo:

1. Subversive Voices in Early Christianity: Amid the male-dominated landscape of early Christianity, women like Thecla and Perpetua emerged as subversive voices. They defied societal expectations, refusing to renounce their faith and demonstrating unwavering commitment to their beliefs.

2. Female Spiritual Leaders in Indigenous Communities: Indigenous communities worldwide have witnessed the leadership of women who serve as healers, spiritual guides, and protectors of cultural heritage. These women have played pivotal roles in preserving ancestral wisdom and traditions.

3. Women as Religious Scholars in Islamic History: Throughout Islamic history, women like Aisha bint Abi Bakr and Fatimah al-Bata'ihiyya became renowned scholars and authorities on religious matters, breaking barriers and leaving a legacy of knowledge.

4. Defenders of Indigenous Spiritual Practices: Women from indigenous cultures have resisted the erasure of their spiritual practices. Women like Winona LaDuke have been at the forefront of reclaiming and preserving indigenous spirituality against the backdrop of colonialism and cultural suppression.

5. Liberation Theologians in Latin America: Women like María Pilar Aquino and Ada María Isasi-Díaz have been instrumental in shaping liberation theology in Latin America. Their work has challenged patriarchal interpretations and emphasized social justice within religious frameworks.

The Importance of Recovering Hidden Narratives:

1. Diverse Role Models: Unearthing hidden narratives introduces a diverse range of role models who defy conventional norms. These stories provide inspiration for present and future generations, showcasing the myriad ways women have contributed to religious and social change.

2. Counteracting Erasure: The recovery of hidden narratives counters the historical erasure of women's contributions. By acknowledging their impact, we challenge the narrative that women's roles have been secondary or insignificant.

3. Broadening Perspective: Hidden narratives broaden our understanding of history and spirituality. They illuminate the complexities of women's experiences and contributions, inviting us to reevaluate our perspectives on gender roles and religious practices.

4. Empowerment and Agency: Recovering hidden narratives empowers women to see themselves as part of a legacy of strength and resistance. These stories remind women that they have the agency to challenge norms and make a lasting impact.

5. Transforming Religious Spaces: Unearthing hidden narratives can reshape religious spaces. By highlighting women's historical agency and leadership, we challenge patriarchal structures and advocate for more inclusive and equitable practices.

In conclusion, uncovering lesser-known stories of women's resistance and leadership is a powerful act of reclaiming history, challenging patriarchal norms, and celebrating the diversity of women's contributions. These narratives serve as beacons of inspiration, encouraging us to question dominant narratives and acknowledge the enduring strength of women in shaping religious and societal landscapes.

Conclusion:

Throughout this exploration, we delved into the intricate relationship between patriarchal religious structures and the resilience of women's resistance and leadership. We navigated the intersections of race and gender oppression, unearthing hidden narratives that challenge conventional historical narratives. The enduring effects of patriarchal norms within religious contexts were illuminated, revealing how they have restricted women's agency, leadership, and spiritual expression.

We witnessed how religious teachings have historically been interpreted to justify gender hierarchy, leading to limitations on women's education, participation in leadership, and decision-making. Racialized misogyny emerged as a distinctive form of discrimination, targeting women of color and further marginalizing their experiences within religious spaces.

Yet, amidst these challenges, we celebrated the stories of women who defied patriarchal norms, demonstrating unwavering strength and courage. We explored the transformative potential of womanism, feminist theology, and liberation movements in challenging oppressive structures and advocating for justice and equity.

Reflecting on the Enduring Effects: The enduring effects of patriarchal religious structures remind us of the deep-rooted nature of these norms. They have shaped cultural attitudes, influenced societal expectations, and often intersected with racial prejudices. The consequences of these structures continue to impact women's lives, limiting their opportunities and stifling their voices.

Encouraging Critical Examination: As we conclude this journey, we encourage readers to critically examine historical narratives and their implications for contemporary gender equity efforts. By unearthing hidden narratives and acknowledging the contributions of women who challenged patriarchal norms, we can reshape the present and future. We urge readers to challenge assumptions, question interpretations, and actively engage in dialogue that transforms religious spaces into more inclusive, just, and equitable environments.

In embracing the stories of women who resisted, led, and defied, we honor their legacy and create space for a more inclusive narrative—one that recognizes the agency and power of all individuals, regardless of their gender or background. Let us move forward with a commitment to dismantling patriarchal religious structures and embracing a future that celebrates the diverse voices that shape our spiritual and societal landscapes.

Chapter 5: Scriptural Interpretations and Gender Bias: Unraveling Harmful Paradigms

Introduction: Exploring Gender Biases in Scriptural Interpretations

In the intricate tapestry of religious traditions, the interpretation of sacred texts holds profound influence over beliefs, practices, and societal norms. However, beneath the surface of these interpretations lies a complex web of gender biases that have historically reinforced and perpetuated inequalities between men and women. This chapter delves into the layers of scriptural interpretations to unveil the gender biases present within them, ultimately urging us to critically examine these biases for the purpose of fostering more equitable understandings.

Emphasizing the Significance: The significance of analyzing the gender biases within scriptural interpretations cannot be overstated. These interpretations have not only shaped religious teachings but have also seeped into broader social frameworks, affecting how gender roles and expectations are perceived. By acknowledging the historical presence of gender biases, we can uncover the mechanisms through which religious texts have been used to maintain patriarchal norms and restrict women's agency.

Highlighting the Importance of Critical Examination: Critical examination becomes a beacon of hope for dismantling these deeply ingrained biases. It is through critical analysis that we gain the ability to challenge established norms, question traditional interpretations, and explore alternative readings that align with principles of justice, equality, and human dignity. By engaging in this process, we open doors to more inclusive and empowering understandings of religious texts, leading us towards a path of greater gender equity.

As we navigate the chapters ahead, we invite you to join us in this journey of exploration and discovery. Together, let us peel back the layers of scriptural interpretations, confront gender biases, and ultimately contribute to a more just and inclusive spiritual landscape.

The Complex Nature of Religious Texts: Navigating Interpretations

Religious texts stand as ancient repositories of wisdom, moral guidance, and spiritual insights. Yet, their interpretations are far from straightforward. These texts, often revered as divine revelations, present a complex tapestry of meanings that intersect with cultural contexts, language nuances, and societal norms. In this chapter, we delve into the intricate nature of religious texts and how their interpretations are shaped by a multitude of factors.

Exploring the Interplay: Cultural Contexts, Language, and Gender Norms:

1. Cultural Contexts: Religious texts are rooted in specific cultural contexts, carrying within them the values, traditions, and norms of their time. The interplay between cultural context and interpretations is evident in how gender roles were perceived and established within societies when these texts were written.

2. Language Nuances: The translation of religious texts introduces a layer of complexity. Language nuances, idioms, and linguistic structures can impact the meaning conveyed, potentially leading to diverse interpretations that affect how gender is portrayed and understood.

3. Gender Norms: Gender norms prevalent during the time of the texts' composition have influenced their portrayal of men and women. Understanding these norms is crucial for discerning whether gender biases are inherent in the text itself or introduced through interpretations.

Highlighting the Role of Historical and Social Factors:

1. Historical Influences: Historical events, societal dynamics, and power structures at the time of the texts' writing can shape the narratives and teachings within them. These factors can impact how gender is addressed and whether it aligns with contemporary gender equity perspectives.

2. Evolving Societal Values: Over time, societal values and norms have evolved, leading to changing interpretations of religious texts. As societies progress towards greater gender equity, interpretations may shift to reflect these advancements.

3. Interpretative Traditions: The interpretative traditions within various religious communities play a pivotal role in shaping how texts are understood. These traditions can reinforce or challenge existing gender norms, depending on the perspectives of scholars and leaders.

Navigating the Layers of Complexity:

The complexity of religious texts necessitates a multi-dimensional approach to interpretation. Recognizing the role of cultural, linguistic, historical, and social factors empowers us to engage with these texts more critically. It enables us to discern between elements that reflect the values of a specific era and those that hold universal ethical teachings.

In the chapters that follow, we will embark on a journey through these intricate layers, analyzing how gender biases have been embedded within scriptural interpretations. By unearthing these biases and fostering a more nuanced understanding of religious texts, we can contribute to a more equitable spiritual discourse that resonates with contemporary values of justice and inclusivity.

Examining Gendered Language and Imagery: Unveiling Hidden Biases

Within the pages of religious texts, the use of language and imagery holds profound implications for how we perceive the divine, human relationships, and societal roles. In this chapter, we embark on an exploration of the gendered language and imagery within these texts, shedding light on the ways in which these linguistic choices have contributed to the perpetuation of patriarchal norms.

Analyzing the Use of Gendered Language:

1. Masculine Terminology: Many religious texts employ masculine terminology to describe the divine or spiritual concepts. This linguistic choice has inadvertently positioned the masculine as the default gender, potentially marginalizing and rendering invisible the divine feminine.

2. Exclusivity: The consistent use of gendered language can exclude those who do not identify with the prescribed gender norms. This exclusion reinforces a binary understanding of gender that disregards the diversity of human experiences.

3. Human Representation: The representation of women and men in religious narratives often reflects societal gender roles of their times. This can lead to reinforcing and perpetuating traditional gender expectations and inequalities.

Discussing How Masculine Terminology Dominates Religious Discourse:

1. Theological Imbalance: The dominance of masculine language and imagery can perpetuate theological imbalances, emphasizing certain aspects of the divine while neglecting others. This imbalance has consequences for how we perceive divine qualities and attributes.

2. Women's Spiritual Identity: The lack of feminine language can impact how women see themselves within religious narratives. The absence of relatable terminology can alienate women from spiritual leadership roles and diminish their sense of belonging.

Exploring the Implications of Gendered Imagery:

1. Shaping Paradigms: Gendered imagery shapes paradigms of power, authority, and hierarchy. When divine figures are exclusively portrayed in masculine terms, this can reinforce hierarchical notions that position the masculine as superior.

2. Reinforcing Gender Norms: Gendered imagery can reinforce traditional gender norms and stereotypes. It has the potential to perpetuate a limited understanding of masculinity and femininity, limiting human potential and diversity.

3. Alternative Narratives: Incorporating diverse gendered imagery opens the door to alternative narratives that challenge patriarchal paradigms. These narratives can promote equity, inclusivity, and a more expansive understanding of the divine.

In the chapters ahead, we will delve deeper into specific examples and contexts, unpacking how gendered language and imagery have influenced religious thought and practice. By critically engaging with these elements, we can illuminate the subtle biases embedded within religious discourse and lay the foundation for a more inclusive, balanced, and transformative spiritual understanding.

Women's Stories and Voices in Scriptures: Rescuing Narratives from Silence

Within the vast tapestry of religious texts, women's stories have often been obscured by the shadows of male-dominated narratives. In this chapter, we embark on a journey to unearth the stories of women found within these texts, understanding their implications, and exploring the efforts to amplify their voices in the face of erasure.

Highlighting Stories of Women:

1. Inspiring Figures: Stories of women in religious texts are not merely anecdotes; they hold profound significance for individuals seeking inspiration and guidance. Women like Esther, Mary Magdalene, and Hagar offer diverse perspectives and demonstrate strength in adversity.

2. Ethical Lessons: Women's stories reveal ethical lessons that transcend time. Their experiences of resilience, sacrifice, and compassion provide invaluable teachings for contemporary audiences.

Discussing Erasure and Marginalization:

1. Traditional Interpretations: Traditional interpretations of religious texts have often marginalized women's voices. Women's roles are minimized, and their agency is downplayed, reinforcing patriarchal norms.

2. Historical Context: The erasure of women's stories often stems from the historical context in which these texts were written. However, this erasure perpetuates the notion that women's experiences are secondary or irrelevant.

Examining Feminist and Womanist Efforts:

1. Feminist Interpretations: Feminist scholars have worked to reclaim women's voices in scripture, challenging traditional interpretations that have silenced them. They reinterpret texts through a gender-conscious lens, unveiling the richness of women's experiences.

2. Womanist Reclamation: Womanist theology emphasizes the significance of women's stories in religious texts, particularly those of Black women and women of color. It seeks to recover these stories to inform contemporary social justice and spirituality.

3. Inclusive Theologies: Efforts to reclaim women's voices align with the broader movement toward inclusive theologies that celebrate diversity and challenge patriarchal structures.

As we delve into the chapters ahead, we will encounter these women's stories, analyze their implications, and explore the transformative power of reclaiming their voices. By celebrating women's experiences and insights, we contribute to a more complete understanding of spirituality and justice, one that honors the stories of all individuals, regardless of their gender.

Disputed Passages and Interpretations: Challenging Harmful Norms

Scriptural passages, revered for their wisdom, have at times been wielded as instruments of oppression against women. In this chapter, we embark on a critical exploration of specific passages that have been used to subjugate women, revealing alternative interpretations that challenge these harmful norms and emphasizing the role of historical context.

Examining Specific Scriptural Passages:

1. Submissive Women: Passages that prescribe submission of women to men have been used to justify gender hierarchy. These passages have been employed to enforce patriarchal norms, relegating women to submissive roles.

2. Women's Silence: Scriptural passages advising women's silence have been weaponized to restrict their participation in religious and public spaces, reinforcing their marginalization.

3. Modesty and Purity: Passages emphasizing women's modesty and purity have been used to control their behavior and reinforce societal expectations regarding their sexuality.

Analyzing Alternative Interpretations:

1. Empowerment Through Submission: Alternative interpretations challenge the literal understanding of submission, asserting that submission should be mutual, rooted in love and respect, and never oppressive.

2. Contextualizing Silence: Alternative interpretations contextualize passages about women's silence, considering the socio-historical context and acknowledging the broader messages of equality and freedom within scripture.

3. Reclaiming Modesty: Alternative interpretations reclaim the concept of modesty to celebrate women's autonomy, highlighting its original intent of self-respect and dignity.

Discussing the Role of Historical Context:

1. Historical Realities: Understanding historical context is crucial for reevaluating contested passages. Scriptures were often written in times vastly different from our own, where social norms were distinct.

2. Evolving Understanding: The evolving understanding of gender equity prompts a reexamination of passages, with a focus on timeless principles that promote justice and equality.

3. Redefining Authority: Contextual interpretations redefine authority, urging us to prioritize overarching principles of compassion, justice, and human dignity.

In the upcoming chapters, we will journey through these contested passages, engage with alternative interpretations, and reflect on the transformative potential of reevaluating these texts. By questioning harmful norms and advocating for inclusive, just readings, we contribute to the creation of a more equitable spiritual narrative that honors the inherent worth and agency of all individuals, regardless of gender.

Feminist and Womanist Reinterpretations: Illuminating Equitable Perspectives

In this chapter, we delve into the transformative contributions of feminist and womanist theologians who have breathed new life into the interpretations of religious texts. Their efforts have paved the way for reimagining scriptures through equitable lenses, challenging oppressive norms, and harnessing the potential for positive change.

Exploring Contributions of Feminist and Womanist Theologians:

1. Unveiling Hidden Voices: Feminist theologians have resurfaced the narratives of overlooked women in scripture, elevating their stories to challenge patriarchal exclusions.

2. Intersectional Insights: Womanist theologians, drawing from the experiences of women of color, offer intersectional analyses that unearth the complexities of gender, race, and social dynamics.

3. Rethinking Divine Imagery: Feminist theologians have questioned the dominantly masculine depictions of the divine, advocating for inclusive and diverse imagery that reflects the full spectrum of human experience.

Discussing Strategies for Equitable Interpretations:

1. Contextual Analysis: Reading scriptures in their historical, cultural, and linguistic contexts allows for a nuanced understanding, revealing messages of justice and equity often obscured by bias.

2. Literary Critique: Employing literary criticism unveils the layers of narratives, shedding light on the roles of women and their significance within the texts.

3. Dialogue and Discussion: Engaging in dialogue and discussion within communities allows for diverse interpretations to emerge, challenging monolithic perspectives and fostering a deeper understanding of scripture.

Highlighting Transformative Potential:

1. Liberation and Empowerment: Equitable interpretations empower marginalized individuals by offering stories of resistance, courage, and agency, reinforcing the values of justice and dignity.

2. Social Change: Inclusive interpretations inspire social change, encouraging believers to challenge unjust norms and systems within their communities.

3. Nurturing Spirituality: Equitable readings enrich spiritual experiences, aligning them with values of compassion, equity, and love, fostering a deeper connection with the divine.

As we journey through these reinterpretations, we recognize the profound impact that feminist and womanist perspectives bring to our understanding of religious texts. By embracing their insights and strategies, we can foster an inclusive spiritual space that resonates with the diverse realities of individuals and promotes a more just, equitable, and transformative religious practice.

Religious Institutions and the Politics of Interpretation: Unraveling Dynamics of Power

In this chapter, we delve into the intricate web of religious institutions and their role in shaping scriptural interpretations. We explore how religious leaders and organizations navigate the terrain of gender biases, and how the dynamics of power and control within these communities influence the narratives that emerge.

Discussing the Authority of Religious Institutions:

1. Interpretative Traditions: Religious institutions hold considerable influence over how scriptures are understood and transmitted. Interpretative traditions, guided by leaders and scholars, shape the lenses through which believers engage with the texts.

2. Orthodoxy and Hierarchy: Orthodox institutions often prioritize established interpretations, reinforcing traditional gender norms and hierarchies. This can perpetuate biases and inhibit transformative interpretations.

Examining Religious Leaders and Gender Biases:

1. Amplifying or Challenging Biases: Religious leaders can play pivotal roles in either perpetuating or challenging gender biases. Their perspectives and teachings can impact believers' understanding of gender roles, justice, and equity.

2. Transformative Leadership: Some religious leaders actively challenge oppressive norms, advocating for gender equality and progressive interpretations. Their leadership can initiate shifts within their communities.

Exploring Dynamics of Power and Control:

1. Patriarchy and Authority: Traditional power structures within religious institutions often reinforce patriarchal norms. Men predominantly occupy leadership positions, influencing decisions and interpretations.

2. Voice and Marginalization: The voices of women and marginalized individuals can be stifled by power dynamics, relegating them to the periphery of discourse and decision-making.

3. Resistance and Change: Despite these challenges, some religious communities engage in resistance against oppressive power dynamics, advocating for greater inclusivity and equity.

As we navigate through these discussions, we uncover the complex interactions between religious institutions, leaders, and interpretations. By acknowledging the authority wielded by these entities, we can foster conversations that challenge biases and encourage a more inclusive, just, and transformative religious landscape.

Conclusion: Envisioning an Equitable Scriptural Landscape

As we conclude our exploration of the intersection of gender and religious texts, we find ourselves at the crossroads of reflection and action. Throughout this journey, we unraveled the layers of gender biases embedded within scriptural interpretations and witnessed the transformative power of reimagining these texts through a gender-equitable lens.

Summarizing the Main Points:

From the complexity of language and imagery to the stories and voices of women in scriptures, we examined how these elements have contributed to gender norms and power dynamics. We navigated the contested passages and celebrated the contributions of feminist and womanist theologians who have enriched our understanding of scripture. We scrutinized the role of religious institutions in shaping interpretations and explored the dynamics of power and resistance within these spaces.

Reflecting on Ongoing Significance:

The significance of reinterpreting religious texts through a gender-equitable lens persists in our contemporary world. As societies evolve and expand their understanding of justice and equality, the reinterpretation of scriptures becomes a dynamic process that aligns with the principles of inclusivity and human dignity.

Encouraging Critical Engagement:

We encourage each reader to engage with religious texts critically, challenging prevailing biases and seeking a more just and equitable interpretation. By questioning, discussing, and contributing to evolving understandings, we contribute to the ongoing transformation of religious discourse.

In embracing the multifaceted interplay between gender and religious texts, we pave the way for a spiritual landscape that celebrates the diversity of human experiences. Let us move forward with a commitment to justice, equality, and empathy, fostering a space where all individuals, regardless of their gender, find resonance, agency, and empowerment.

Navigating Historical Backlash Against Womanism

In this chapter, we delve into the annals of history to uncover instances of religious backlash against womanism—an unyielding movement advocating for the rights, agency, and liberation of women. As we journey through these historical landscapes, we will confront the challenges faced by womanist activists and thinkers, while recognizing the enduring strength and resistance that have characterized their path.

Exploring Historical Backlash:

1. Silencing Dissent: Throughout history, womanist thought has often been met with resistance from traditional religious institutions seeking to maintain the status quo. Backlash has taken various forms, from subtle marginalization to outright suppression.

2. Opposing Liberation: Womanism's radical call for gender equity, racial justice, and social transformation has sometimes been met with opposition from religious authorities seeking to preserve hierarchical power structures.

Highlighting Challenges and Resistance:

1. Womanist Activists: Womanist activists have faced challenges ranging from excommunication to character assassination. Yet, their resilience and determination have kept the flame of womanism burning bright.

2. Marginalization and Misrepresentation: Womanist thinkers have grappled with being marginalized within religious spaces and misinterpreted by dominant religious narratives. Their efforts to challenge norms often led to their voices being dismissed or distorted.

Emphasizing Historical Context:

1. Contextual Understanding: Acknowledging the historical context of womanism's struggles is essential for appreciating the magnitude of their achievements and the obstacles they surmounted.

2. Lessons from the Past: Examining historical instances of backlash provides valuable insights into the mechanisms used to stifle progress and offers guidance for navigating similar challenges today.

As we embark on this exploration of historical backlash, let us honor the courage of womanist activists and thinkers who confronted adversity head-on. Their stories illuminate the path forward, reminding us of the importance of perseverance and solidarity in the face of resistance.

Historical Instances of Religious Opposition: Tracing Womanism's Journey

In this chapter, we delve into the annals of history to unearth poignant examples of religious institutions opposing the womanist movement. These instances not only shed light on the challenges womanist activists faced but also reveal the tactics employed by religious authorities to suppress and silence their voices.

Discussing Historical Examples:

1. Suffrage Movements: Womanist activists advocating for gender equity and women's suffrage often encountered opposition from religious institutions that upheld traditional gender roles and power dynamics.

2. Civil Rights Era: As womanism emerged alongside the Civil Rights Movement, some religious leaders resisted the intersectional approach of womanism, preferring a narrower focus on racial justice.

Examining Silencing and Marginalization:

1. Excommunication: Womanist thinkers who challenged traditional religious norms and practices were sometimes excommunicated, marking their dissent as unacceptable within established religious frameworks.

2. Distortion of Message: Religious institutions sometimes distorted womanist narratives, misrepresenting their goals and ideas, in order to discredit and undermine their credibility.

Highlighting Societal and Cultural Shifts:

1. Patriarchal Norms: Historical religious opposition often stemmed from deeply entrenched patriarchal norms that sought to maintain male authority and suppress women's agency.

2. Shifting Gender Roles: As society underwent changes in gender roles, some religious institutions resisted womanism as a perceived threat to their traditional power structures.

3. Racial Dynamics: The intersectional nature of womanism, addressing both gender and racial justice, sometimes challenged racial hierarchies upheld within religious communities.

These historical instances of religious opposition remind us of the resilience of womanist activists and the uphill battles they faced in pursuit of justice and equity. By understanding the strategies employed by religious institutions to suppress womanism, we can better navigate present challenges and work towards dismantling oppressive systems that persist today.

Womanism's Response to Religious Backlash: Navigating Uncharted Waters

In this chapter, we delve into the remarkable strategies womanists employed to navigate the treacherous waters of religious opposition. Through resilience, courage, and unwavering commitment, they challenged and dismantled barriers while leaving an indelible mark on the landscape of gender justice and religious discourse.

Exploring Womanist Strategies:

1. Reclamation of Scriptures: Womanists engaged in reinterpreting religious texts from an intersectional perspective, uncovering narratives of resilience and liberation that had been overlooked or suppressed.

2. Intersectional Solidarity: Womanists embraced intersectionality, forging alliances with diverse social justice movements to create a united front against oppressive religious structures.

3. The Power of Storytelling: Womanists utilized storytelling to share experiences of resistance, transforming personal narratives into collective empowerment.

Resilience and Tenacity:

1. Unwavering Advocacy: Despite facing excommunication, marginalization, and hostility, womanists stood their ground, advocating for justice and equity within their religious communities.

2. Academic Contributions: Womanist scholars tirelessly produced rigorous research and writings that unveiled the intersections of gender, race, and spirituality, challenging normative religious narratives.

Challenging Religious Institutions:

1. From Within: Some womanists worked to transform religious institutions from within, pushing for gender-inclusive leadership and theology that aligned with their values.

2. Advocacy from Without: Others advocated from outside traditional religious institutions, using their voices and platforms to amplify the call for gender justice and liberation.

As we explore womanism's response to religious backlash, let us be inspired by their audacious resolve and transformative strategies. By understanding their methods, we can apply their lessons to current struggles, building a more inclusive and just spiritual space for all individuals, irrespective of their gender or background.

Religious Resistance to Change: Unveiling the Status Quo

In this chapter, we delve into the complex phenomenon of religious resistance to change, particularly in the context of evolving gender norms. We explore how conservatism within religious institutions has impeded progress and analyze the ways in which these institutions have resisted acknowledging their complicity in perpetuating gender-based oppression.

Examining Reluctance to Adapt:

1. Clinging to Tradition: Religious institutions, rooted in centuries-old traditions, can be resistant to adapting to changing gender norms. This resistance stems from a desire to maintain established power dynamics.

2. Fear of Disruption: The fear of disrupting the status quo and altering perceived divine order leads to hesitation in embracing gender equity within religious structures.

Discussing Conservatism's Impact:

1. Stifling Progress: Conservatism within religious communities can stifle efforts to challenge oppressive gender norms. This inhibits the potential for religious institutions to evolve and promote justice.

2. Reinforcing Hierarchies: Conservative ideologies often reinforce patriarchal hierarchies, making it difficult to acknowledge and address the systemic gender-based inequalities present within these institutions.

Analyzing Resistance to Acknowledge Complicity:

1. Cognitive Dissonance: Religious institutions may resist acknowledging their complicity in gender-based oppression due to cognitive dissonance between their stated values and the reality of their practices.

2. Defense of Tradition: Acknowledging complicity may be seen as an attack on tradition, causing institutions to double down on justifying practices that uphold gender-based oppression.

As we navigate the complexities of religious resistance to change, we recognize the need to approach this challenge with nuance and empathy. By understanding the dynamics at play, we can engage in meaningful conversations that encourage religious institutions to grapple with their role in perpetuating gender inequality and take meaningful steps toward equity and justice.

Impact on Leadership and Representation: Navigating Gendered Pathways

In this chapter, we delve into the intricate dynamics surrounding womanist leaders within religious organizations, as well as the broader challenges tied to limited representation of women in religious leadership roles. We explore the hurdles faced by these leaders and underscore the transformative potential of diverse leadership in challenging and reshaping religious gender norms.

Discussing Challenges Faced by Womanist Leaders:

1. Glass Ceiling: Womanist leaders often encounter barriers that impede their advancement into higher leadership positions within religious institutions, perpetuating gender hierarchies.

2. Marginalization: Womanist leaders may face marginalization, their voices and insights dismissed or undervalued due to the intersectionality of their perspectives.

Examining Limited Representation:

1. Traditional Norms: Limited representation of women in religious leadership is often rooted in traditional gender norms that assign women to subordinate roles.

2. Cultural Constructs: Societal constructs that define leadership as masculine further contribute to the underrepresentation of women in religious leadership roles.

Highlighting Transformative Potential of Diverse Leadership:

1. Challenging Norms: Diverse womanist leadership challenges established gender norms and expands the range of acceptable roles for women within religious institutions.

2. Expanding Narratives: Diverse leadership narratives expand the understanding of spirituality, drawing from a wider range of perspectives and experiences.

3. Transforming Discourse: Womanist leaders offer alternative theological perspectives that reshape discussions around gender, justice, and spirituality.

As we navigate the complexities of leadership and representation within religious contexts, let us recognize the urgency of promoting equitable leadership pathways. By fostering a diverse array of leaders, we challenge existing norms and propel religious institutions toward more inclusive, just, and transformative spaces for all believers.

The Role of Intersectionality in Resilience: Weaving Threads of Strength

In this chapter, we delve into the integral role of intersectionality in womanist responses to religious backlash. We explore the ways in which the interconnectedness of race, gender, and faith shapes womanist resistance, and we celebrate the contributions of womanists from marginalized backgrounds in shaping the movement's strategies.

Exploring Intersectionality's Depth:

1. Multi-Dimensional Challenges: Womanists confront challenges that emerge at the intersections of their gender, race, and faith identities, leading to a unique and complex experience of religious backlash.

2. Uniting Struggles: Intersectionality unites womanist activists across various social justice movements, allowing them to identify shared struggles and advocate for equitable change.

Discussing Interconnectedness:

1. Inseparable Bonds: Race, gender, and faith are inseparably intertwined within the womanist experience, shaping their understanding of justice, resilience, and spirituality.

2. Triple Oppression: Intersectionality exposes the triple oppression that many womanists face—oppression due to their race, gender, and the intersection of the two.

Highlighting Contributions of Marginalized Womanists:

1. Nuanced Strategies: Womanists from marginalized backgrounds bring nuanced strategies to the movement, drawing from their experiences to craft resilience and resistance tactics.

2. Empowerment through Unity: Collaborations between marginalized womanists bolster solidarity, amplifying their collective power to enact change within religious institutions.

As we journey through the intersectional landscape of womanist responses to religious backlash, let us appreciate the strength drawn from the interconnected threads of identity. By understanding the profound impact of intersectionality, we affirm the diversity and complexity that make womanism a forceful movement for justice, equity, and transformation.

Collaboration and Solidarity: Weaving a Web of Empowerment

In this chapter, we delve into the remarkable collaborations and solidarities that have fortified womanist activists, extending beyond religious contexts. We explore the cross-movement alliances for social justice and equality that womanists have fostered and examine how these bonds of solidarity have strengthened womanism's stance against religious backlash.

Discussing Collaborations Beyond Religious Contexts:

1. Uniting Across Movements: Womanist activists have extended their alliances beyond religious spaces, forming partnerships with feminist, LGBTQ+, racial justice, and other social justice movements.

2. Amplifying Intersectionality: Collaborations highlight the intersectional nature of womanism, connecting various struggles under the shared banner of justice and equity.

Exploring Cross-Movement Collaborations:

1. Shared Goals: Womanists have recognized shared goals in various movements, such as dismantling systemic oppression, challenging gender norms, and advocating for marginalized voices.

2. Strength in Unity: Collaborations amplify the collective power of social justice movements, showcasing the potential for transformative change on multiple fronts.

Analyzing Solidarity's Impact:

1. Resilience and Resonance: Solidarity across movements provides womanists with a resilient support system that validates their experiences and empowers their resistance.

2. Broadening Influence: Solidarity amplifies womanism's influence beyond religious spheres, fostering greater awareness and engagement with its principles.

As we delve into the tapestry of collaboration and solidarity, let us embrace the profound impact that unified efforts can have in dismantling oppression and fostering justice. By weaving connections that transcend boundaries, womanists create a rich network of empowerment that can navigate the challenges of religious backlash and beyond.

Conclusion: Lessons from History's Tapestry of Resilience

As we conclude our exploration into the historical challenges and resilience of womanist activists amidst religious opposition, we find ourselves standing at the crossroads of reflection and action. Throughout this journey, we uncovered the unwavering determination of womanist activists, their collaborative spirit, and their steadfast resistance against religious barriers.

Summarizing the Main Points:

From navigating religious backlash and opposition to challenging traditional norms, we traced the contours of womanism's historical journey. We explored intersectional strategies, diverse leadership, and collaborative efforts that have propelled womanism forward in the face of adversity.

Reflecting on Historical Challenges and Resilience:

The historical challenges womanist activists confronted served as crucibles of resilience, igniting fires of change that continue to burn bright. These challenges fortified their resolve, inspiring generations to follow suit in the ongoing pursuit of justice and liberation.

Encouraging Ongoing Struggles for Justice:

As we reflect on the lessons of history, let us draw inspiration from the tenacity of womanist activists who carved paths of progress amidst resistance. Let their stories inspire our commitment to contribute, in our own ways, to the ongoing struggles for justice and liberation.

By engaging with womanism's history, we stand poised to embrace the present and shape the future. Let us celebrate the victories, learn from the challenges, and unite in the pursuit of a more just, equitable, and inclusive world—where the spirit of womanism and its resilience continue to be a beacon of hope for all.

Introduction: Womanist Strategies Against Religious Oppression

In this chapter, we embark on a journey into the heart of womanist strategies for resisting religious oppression. We delve into the empowering and courageous tactics that womanists employ as they navigate the complex intersection of gender, race, and faith. Through their agency and resilience, womanists challenge the norms that perpetuate inequality and work toward justice and equity.

Exploring Empowerment and Agency:

1. Reclaiming Identity: Womanists reclaim their agency by refusing to be defined solely by religious norms that perpetuate oppression. They recognize their power to reshape narratives that have marginalized them.

2. Challenging Boundaries: Womanists challenge the boundaries that religious institutions impose on their roles and contributions, asserting their right to leadership, theology, and interpretation.

Emphasizing Resilience in Adversity:

1. Navigating Resistance: Womanists confront resistance and hostility with a determination that refuses to be silenced. They draw strength from their spiritual convictions and forge ahead with courage.

2. Transforming Adversity: In the face of adversity, womanists are adept at transforming challenges into opportunities for growth and change. Their resilience is a testament to their unwavering commitment to justice.

As we delve into the strategies womanists employ to resist religious oppression, let us be inspired by their agency, empowered by their resistance, and reminded that in the pursuit of justice and equity, every step forward is a victory.

Recognition of Intersectional Identities: Navigating Complexities with Womanism

In this chapter, we delve into the profound significance of acknowledging intersectionality within womanist activism. We explore how womanists adeptly navigate the intricate web of overlapping systems of oppression, demonstrating the power of recognizing and embracing their multiple identities in the pursuit of justice.

Discussing Importance of Intersectionality:

1. Holistic Understanding: Acknowledging intersectionality in womanist activism allows for a holistic understanding of how various forms of oppression intertwine and impact individuals.

2. Amplifying Voices: Intersectionality amplifies the voices of those who experience compounded oppression, ensuring that no one's struggles are silenced or overlooked.

Exploring Navigating Overlapping Oppression:

1. Deconstructing Systems: Womanists deconstruct oppressive systems by recognizing how racism, sexism, and other forms of discrimination intersect and create unique challenges.

2. Resisting Compartmentalization: Instead of compartmentalizing their experiences, womanists understand the interconnectedness of their identities and strive for collective liberation.

Highlighting Resilience through Identity Recognition:

1. Fostering Empathy: Recognizing one's intersectional identity fosters empathy and solidarity with others facing similar challenges, leading to a stronger sense of community.

2. Fueling Resilience: Embracing intersectionality fuels the resilience needed to overcome adversity, as womanists draw strength from the diverse aspects of their identity.

As we delve into the realm of intersectionality within womanism, let us be inspired by the ways in which embracing the complexities of identity enhances our understanding of the multifaceted struggle for justice and equity. By recognizing the power of intersectionality, womanists provide a roadmap for dismantling systems of oppression and fostering a more inclusive and empathetic world.

In a world where religious oppression has often targeted women, there exist remarkable narratives of womanist resilience and triumph. These stories are testaments to the unyielding spirit of women who have defied religious constraints to rise above adversity. Through their determination, these women have not only broken free from oppressive systems but also inspired others with their strategies and approaches. This article explores real-life examples of such women and delves into the ways they overcame religious oppression.

1. Malala Yousafzai: Education as Liberation Malala Yousafzai, a Pakistani activist, stood against the oppressive grip of the Taliban on education. In defiance of their ban on girls' education, Malala continued attending school and eventually became an advocate for education rights. Her activism culminated in a tragic attack in 2012, where she was shot in the head by the Taliban. Despite this horrific event, Malala survived and continued her campaign for girls' education, eventually becoming the youngest Nobel Prize laureate. Her story showcases the power of education as a means of liberation from religious oppression.

2. Amina Wadud: Redefining Women's Role in Islam Amina Wadud, an American scholar and Muslim feminist, challenged traditional interpretations of Islamic texts that limited women's roles within the religion. Through her scholarship and activism, she advocated for a more inclusive understanding of Islam that empowers women. In 2005, she led a mixed-gender Friday prayer in New York, sparking discussions about women's leadership in religious spaces. Wadud's determination to reinterpret religious teachings showcases how women can reshape religious narratives to empower themselves.

3. Asmaa Mahfouz: The Voice of the Egyptian Revolution Asmaa Mahfouz, an Egyptian activist, harnessed the power of social media to galvanize the masses during the 2011 Egyptian Revolution. As a devout Muslim woman, she overcame societal expectations to play a pivotal role in inspiring protests that led to the downfall of the oppressive regime. Her courage in the face of religious and gender-based oppression demonstrates how women can use modern tools to challenge traditional power structures.

4. Sikh Women Challenging Patriarchy Sikhism, a religion known for its commitment to equality, has also faced instances of gender-based discrimination. Sikh women like Balpreet Kaur have challenged societal norms by embracing their faith while rejecting oppressive practices. Balpreet, for instance, responded gracefully to online harassment about her facial hair, educating her critics about Sikh beliefs. Sikh women's resilience within their own faith exemplifies how religious traditions can be reclaimed to empower women.

5. Shirin Ebadi: Women's Rights in Iran Shirin Ebadi, an Iranian lawyer and former judge, fought tirelessly for women's rights and human rights in Iran. Despite facing persecution and exile due to her advocacy, she never wavered in her commitment to justice. Ebadi's story underscores the importance of legal activism in challenging oppressive religious regimes and advancing women's rights.

The narratives of womanist resilience and triumph against religious oppression illustrate the indomitable spirit of women who refuse to be constrained by oppressive norms. Through education, reinterpretation of religious texts, technological innovation, reclaiming traditions, and legal activism, these women have shown that overcoming adversity is possible. Their stories inspire us to continue challenging religious oppression and fostering environments where women can thrive and lead without barriers.

Challenging Religious Norms

Challenging oppressive religious norms requires courage, determination, and a deep commitment to justice. Womanists, who center the experiences of women of color within religious contexts, have developed powerful strategies to challenge and transform harmful beliefs within their faith communities. This article delves into the ways womanists navigate religious spaces, employ theological arguments, and engage critical thinking to dismantle oppressive norms.

1. Activism Within Religious Spaces and Institutions Womanist activists often choose to remain within their religious communities to foster change from within. By challenging oppressive norms within the very spaces they belong to, these women reclaim their agency and influence. They organize discussions, workshops, and awareness campaigns that address issues such as gender-based discrimination, LGBTQ+ inclusion, and reproductive rights. This strategy enables them to challenge harmful beliefs while maintaining a connection to their faith.

2. Reinterpretation and Theological Arguments Womanists engage in deep theological reflection to reinterpret religious texts and challenge patriarchal interpretations. They seek out alternative readings that amplify the voices of marginalized individuals and unveil the underlying principles of justice and equality within their faiths. By using theological arguments, womanists undermine oppressive norms with the very tools that have been historically used to uphold them.

3. Critical Thinking and Intersectionality Womanists apply critical thinking to dissect and analyze religious teachings, exposing inconsistencies and biases that perpetuate oppressive norms. They also recognize the intersections of race, gender, class, and other identities, understanding that oppression is interconnected. By highlighting these intersections, womanists emphasize the need for a more holistic and inclusive approach to religious understanding.

4. Ritual Innovation and Inclusion Challenging oppressive religious norms often involves reimagining rituals and practices to be more inclusive and affirming of women's experiences. Womanists creatively adapt traditional ceremonies, prayers, and rituals to reflect the evolving roles and identities of women within their communities. This process not only challenges gender-based restrictions but also reinvigorates the faith with a renewed sense of purpose.

5. Building Supportive Networks Womanists create networks of support within and across different faith communities, fostering a sense of solidarity. These networks provide a safe space for sharing experiences, ideas, and strategies for challenging oppressive norms. By amplifying each other's voices, womanists strengthen their collective influence and create a united front against religious oppression.

Womanists embody the spirit of resilience and transformation as they challenge oppressive religious norms. Through activism within religious spaces, reinterpreting theology, applying critical thinking, reimagining rituals, and building supportive networks, they carve a path toward more inclusive, just, and equitable faith communities. By sharing their narratives and strategies, womanists inspire others to join the movement for positive change within religious institutions and beyond.

Reclaiming Spiritual Spaces

Spiritual spaces have often been arenas where oppressive norms have marginalized and silenced women. However, womanists have embarked on a journey of reclamation, using these spaces to empower themselves and affirm their identities. This article delves into the ways womanists reclaim spiritual spaces, revive rituals, ceremonies, and practices, and leverage spirituality to foster resilience and healing.

1. Reclaiming Rituals and Ceremonies Womanists reclaim rituals and ceremonies that have historically excluded or diminished the voices of women. By revisiting these traditions, they infuse them with new meaning that reflects their identities and experiences. For example, rituals related to childbirth, marriage, and coming of age can be adapted to honor womanist values of equality, agency, and empowerment.

2. Reviving Forgotten Practices Through historical research and oral traditions, womanists unearth forgotten practices that celebrate women's roles in spirituality. These practices might include herbal healing, storytelling, and artistic expressions that honor the sacred feminine. By revitalizing these customs, womanists reconnect with their heritage and forge a deeper connection to their spirituality.

3. Centering Inclusivity Womanists transform spiritual spaces into inclusive environments where diverse experiences are celebrated. They challenge exclusionary language, imagery, and practices, making these spaces welcoming to people of all genders, sexual orientations, and backgrounds. This inclusivity not only affirms womanist identities but also fosters a sense of belonging and unity.

4. Embracing Earth-Based Spirituality Many womanists turn to earth-based spiritual practices that emphasize interconnectedness, sustainability, and the sacredness of nature. These practices enable them to reconnect with their roots, honor ancestral wisdom, and draw strength from the land. Earth-based spirituality becomes a conduit for healing and empowerment.

5. Spirituality as a Source of Resilience and Healing Spiritual practices provide womanists with tools to navigate challenges and trauma. Prayer, meditation, and reflection help them tap into inner strength and resilience. Moreover, spirituality offers a platform for healing from past wounds, enabling womanists to reclaim agency over their lives and narratives.

6. Rituals of Empowerment Womanists create new rituals that celebrate milestones, achievements, and personal growth. These rituals mark moments of triumph over adversity and serve as reminders of womanist resilience. They contribute to a sense of empowerment and self-worth, bolstering womanists' determination to challenge oppressive norms.

The reclamation of spiritual spaces by womanists exemplifies the transformative power of embracing one's heritage, rewriting narratives, and fostering healing. By infusing rituals, ceremonies, and practices with womanist values, these empowered individuals not only redefine their relationship with spirituality but also inspire others to do the same. Through this reclamation, womanists pave the way for a future where spiritual spaces are inclusive, empowering, and affirming of all identities.

Community Building and Mutual Support

Community building is a cornerstone of womanist resistance, providing a platform for mutual support, solidarity, and collective action. In the face of religious oppression, womanists have harnessed the power of community to amplify their voices and challenge harmful norms. This article examines the significance of community in womanist resistance, the ways they establish networks of support, and the role of collective action in dismantling religious oppression.

1. The Power of Community Community plays a vital role in womanist resistance, offering a space where shared experiences are acknowledged and validated. These spaces empower womanists to express themselves authentically, without fear of judgment or marginalization. Through communal bonds, womanists find strength, affirmation, and a collective sense of purpose.

2. Creating Networks of Support Womanists intentionally create networks of support that span across religious, cultural, and geographical boundaries. These networks provide a safe haven for sharing stories, seeking advice, and fostering connections with like-minded individuals. Online platforms, social media, and gatherings enable womanists to bridge gaps and establish a global network of solidarity.

3. Fostering Solidarity and Intersectionality Womanists understand the importance of intersectionality in their resistance efforts. They recognize the interconnected nature of different forms of oppression and actively work to build bridges with other marginalized communities. By fostering solidarity and embracing diverse perspectives, womanists strengthen their collective impact.

4. Amplifying Marginalized Voices Collective action within womanist communities amplifies the voices of marginalized individuals, drawing attention to issues that have long been silenced. Through joint advocacy efforts, campaigns, and protests, womanists raise awareness about religious oppression and push for change on a larger scale.

5. Challenging Religious Norms Through Unity Collective action enables womanists to challenge oppressive religious norms from a position of strength. By pooling their resources, knowledge, and skills, they can strategize and enact change within their religious spaces. This unity serves as a counterforce against those who seek to maintain the status quo.

6. Inspiring Empowerment and Resilience Communities provide a supportive environment for womanists to share stories of triumph over religious oppression. These success stories inspire others to take action, fostering a sense of empowerment and resilience within the collective. By celebrating each other's victories, womanists create a cycle of positive change.

Community building stands at the heart of womanist resistance, offering a space where shared experiences are honored, and collective action is forged. Through networks of support, solidarity, and collective efforts, womanists challenge oppressive religious norms and pave the way for a more inclusive, just, and equitable future. As womanists continue to strengthen their bonds, their impact on dismantling religious oppression continues to grow, inspiring others to join the movement for positive change.

Educational Initiatives and Advocacy

Educational initiatives and advocacy are powerful tools that womanists wield to challenge religious oppression and foster positive change. Womanist scholars and activists are at the forefront of raising awareness, advocating for reform, and reshaping theological discourse. This article explores the impact of womanist educational initiatives, the role of womanist scholars in advocacy, and their contributions to critical engagement within religious contexts.

1. Raising Awareness through Educational Initiatives Womanist educational initiatives serve as platforms to raise awareness about the intersection of gender, race, and religion. Workshops, seminars, and online resources provide spaces for individuals to learn about the unique experiences of womanists and the challenges they face within their religious communities. These initiatives create informed allies and foster empathy, driving the movement for change forward.

2. Womanist Scholars as Advocates for Change Womanist scholars play a crucial role in advocating for change within religious institutions. They use their expertise to challenge oppressive interpretations of religious texts, traditions, and practices. By engaging in critical analysis, they expose the ways in which patriarchal and discriminatory norms have been historically perpetuated, and propose alternative interpretations that empower marginalized groups.

3. Reshaping Theological Discourse Womanist scholars contribute to theological discourse by centering the experiences of women of color and highlighting their unique perspectives. They engage in rigorous research, writing, and speaking engagements that challenge conventional wisdom and elevate the voices of those traditionally marginalized. Through their work, they transform the conversation around religious beliefs and practices.

4. Bridging the Gap between Academia and Activism Womanist scholars bridge the gap between academic research and on-the-ground activism. They translate complex ideas into accessible language, making their insights applicable to a broader audience. By offering guidance, resources, and tools for change, they empower individuals to take action within their own religious communities.

5. Cultivating Critical Engagement Womanist scholars encourage critical engagement with religious teachings, urging individuals to question oppressive norms. They create spaces for dialogue where people can challenge harmful beliefs, explore alternative interpretations, and contribute to the ongoing process of reshaping religious understanding. This critical engagement fosters growth, evolution, and inclusivity.

6. Advocacy for Structural Change Womanist scholars advocate for structural changes within religious institutions that promote gender equity and social justice. They call for the inclusion of women's voices in leadership roles, the revision of exclusionary practices, and the establishment of policies that uphold equality. Their advocacy has the potential to reshape religious institutions from the inside out.

Womanist educational initiatives, advocacy, and scholarly contributions are catalysts for dismantling religious oppression and fostering positive change. By raising awareness, reshaping theological discourse, and advocating for structural reform, womanists create a more inclusive and equitable religious landscape. Their efforts inspire individuals to critically engage with their faith, challenge harmful norms, and contribute to the ongoing movement for justice and equality.

In this chapter, we explored the dynamic strategies employed by womanists to resist religious oppression, drawing inspiration from their resilience and triumphs. The multifaceted approaches discussed shed light on their relentless pursuit of justice and liberation within religious contexts.

Main Points:

- **Narratives of Resilience and Triumph:** We delved into real-life examples of womanist figures who defied religious constraints, such as Malala Yousafzai, Amina Wadud, Asmaa Mahfouz, and others. These stories showcased their determination and the power of education, reinterpreted theology, and technological innovation to overcome religious oppression.
- **Challenging Religious Norms:** Womanists creatively challenged oppressive religious norms by actively engaging with their faith communities. They used theological arguments, critical thinking, and ritual innovation to challenge harmful beliefs and redefine the roles of women within religious spaces.
- **Reclaiming Spiritual Spaces:** The chapter highlighted how womanists reclaim spiritual spaces for empowerment. By reinterpreting rituals, reviving forgotten practices, and embracing earth-based spirituality, they fostered healing and reaffirmed their identities within their faiths.
- **Community Building and Mutual Support:** Womanists emphasized the significance of community in their resistance efforts. They built networks of support and solidarity, fostering inclusive environments that amplified marginalized voices and inspired collective action.

- **Educational Initiatives and Advocacy:** Womanist scholars played a pivotal role in reshaping theological discourse and advocating for change. Through educational initiatives, they raised awareness about the intersections of gender, race, and religion, bridging the gap between academia and activism.

Reflection and Encouragement:

The multifaceted strategies employed by womanists provide a rich tapestry of inspiration for readers to draw from. The resilience, innovation, and tenacity demonstrated by these women can serve as guiding lights for anyone seeking justice and liberation in their own contexts. By embracing education, critical thinking, collective action, and community support, individuals can apply womanist principles to their efforts, effecting positive change within their communities and beyond.

As we reflect on the chapters shared narratives, let us remember that change is possible, even in the face of deep-rooted religious oppression. By learning from womanists' narratives of resilience, we can carry their torch of empowerment into our own endeavors, contributing to a world that embraces diversity, equality, and justice for all.

Chapter 8: Healing the Divide: Womanist Rituals and
Spiritual Empowerment

Introduction: Empowering Healing through Womanist Rituals

Within the tapestry of womanist resistance, rituals emerge as
profound tools for healing, empowerment, and reclamation. This
chapter embarks on a journey into the realm of womanist rituals,
exploring their significance in restoring spirituality, confronting
oppressive norms, and nurturing individual and collective well-being.
As women of color challenge religious constraints and forge pathways
of empowerment, rituals stand as transformative acts that carry the
weight of tradition and the promise of a liberated future.

**Reclaiming Spirituality and Challenging Oppression: The Power
of Rituals**

Rituals serve as potent acts of defiance against oppressive religious
norms. By engaging in rituals that have been historically marginalized
or silenced, womanists reclaim their spiritual identities with a fervent
determination. These rituals become channels through which the
sacred is redefined and the limitations of traditional interpretations
are challenged. As womanists reshape rituals to reflect their values of
equality, agency, and inclusivity, they enact a quiet revolution against
deeply ingrained oppressive structures.

**Nurturing Well-being through Womanist Rituals: Healing and
Empowerment**

At the heart of womanist rituals lies a profound commitment to healing and empowerment. These rituals offer safe spaces for individuals to process trauma, confront past injustices, and find solace in the embrace of their spiritual heritage. Womanist rituals, rooted in a deep understanding of the intersections of race, gender, and spirituality, foster individual well-being by validating experiences and facilitating emotional release.

Moreover, womanist rituals extend their influence to the collective sphere, creating a network of shared experiences and collective healing. Through communal engagement in these rituals, womanists forge bonds of solidarity, where pain and joy are woven into a tapestry of resilience. The act of coming together to celebrate, mourn, or transform becomes a vessel through which womanists nurture their communities and draw strength from one another.

Empowering Narratives of Liberation through Rituals

As we embark on this exploration of womanist rituals, we are invited to witness the profound ways in which women of color wield these practices to reclaim spirituality, challenge oppressive norms, and foster healing and empowerment. In the rich tapestry of womanist resistance, rituals stand as vibrant threads, weaving a narrative of liberation and transformation. Through their acts of reclamation, womanists illuminate a path towards a future where spirituality is inclusive, justice is paramount, and rituals are vehicles of empowerment for all.

Reclaiming Spirituality through Womanist Rituals

In the journey of womanist empowerment, rituals stand as profound instruments of reclaiming spirituality. These rituals, intentionally designed to challenge oppressive norms, play a pivotal role in reconnecting individuals with their spiritual heritage, fostering healing, and rewriting narratives of faith. Through deliberate acts of ceremony and celebration, womanists breathe life into ancient practices, infusing them with their own identities and aspirations.

Reconnecting with Ancestral Wisdom: The Significance of Rituals

Womanist rituals serve as a bridge to ancestral wisdom that has often been obscured by oppressive narratives. By embracing rituals that have been passed down through generations, womanists reconnect with their roots, retrieving cultural and spiritual wisdom that holds profound relevance for contemporary challenges. These rituals become vessels through which womanists revive traditions, revitalize collective memory, and honor the legacies of those who came before them.

Challenging Patriarchal and Colonial Narratives: Rituals as Acts of Resistance

Rituals, as acts of resistance, offer womanists a means to challenge patriarchal and colonial religious narratives that have marginalized their voices. Through the intentional subversion of traditional practices, womanists reinterpret rituals to reflect their own values, experiences, and identities. These acts of creative defiance serve as powerful statements against the erasure of women's stories and perspectives within religious contexts.

Reimagining Sacred Spaces: Rituals as Sites of Transformation

Womanist rituals hold the power to transform spaces traditionally dominated by patriarchal and colonial influences. As womanists gather to perform rituals that celebrate the sacred feminine, they reshape religious spaces, asserting their presence and agency. These transformed spaces become arenas where womanists reclaim their identities, renegotiate their roles, and challenge the exclusivity of historical religious practices.

Womanist Rituals as Agents of Transformation

In the tapestry of womanist resistance, rituals emerge as agents of transformation, reclamation, and subversion. Through their intentional engagement with rituals, womanists rewrite the narrative of spirituality, rekindling a connection with ancestral wisdom, challenging oppressive narratives, and reshaping sacred spaces. As womanists employ these rituals to empower themselves and their communities, they create a vibrant, inclusive, and evolving spiritual tapestry that celebrates the strength, resilience, and diversity of women of color.

Rituals of Healing and Resilience: Nurturing Womanist Well-being

In the journey of womanist empowerment, rituals take on a profound role as conduits for healing, resilience, and self-affirmation. These rituals serve as transformative spaces where women of color can confront the traumas of oppression, mend emotional wounds, and reclaim agency over their identities. By engaging in practices that prioritize emotional and psychological well-being, womanists cultivate resilience and forge pathways towards liberation.

Confronting Trauma through Rituals: Embracing Healing

Womanist rituals offer a sanctuary for confronting the traumas that systemic oppression has inflicted upon individuals and communities. Rituals of storytelling, communal sharing, and guided reflection provide spaces where pain can be acknowledged, shared, and ultimately transformed. These rituals validate experiences, fostering a sense of collective solidarity while nurturing individual healing.

Fostering Emotional and Psychological Well-being: Nurturing the Self

Central to womanist rituals is the nurturing of emotional and psychological well-being. Practices of meditation, self-care, and mindfulness are integrated into rituals to offer participants tools for centering themselves, acknowledging their emotions, and promoting self-awareness. These rituals encourage a sense of agency and self-worth, reminding women of color of their intrinsic value and resilience.

Examples of Empowering Rituals: Reclaiming Agency

Womanist rituals are as diverse as the individuals who engage in them. For instance, a ritual of "speaking back" allows participants to voice their experiences of oppression, reclaiming the narrative that was once controlled by others. Rituals involving art, music, and dance become expressions of self-love, defiance, and empowerment, transforming pain into creative energy.

Empowering Resilience through Womanist Rituals

Womanist rituals emerge as vital spaces for nurturing healing, emotional well-being, and resilience. These rituals create pathways towards self-empowerment and collective liberation, enabling women of color to confront trauma, reclaim agency, and rewrite the stories of their lives. By engaging in rituals that honor their experiences, womanists pave the way for healing that ripples through their communities, fostering strength and transformation.

Rituals of Empowerment and Solidarity: Uniting Through Womanist Rituals

Within the tapestry of womanist empowerment, rituals stand as vibrant threads that weave empowerment and solidarity into the fabric of women's lives. These intentional rituals celebrate achievements, amplify strength, and nurture a sense of community, fostering bonds of sisterhood that transcend boundaries and amplify the collective spirit of women of color.

Celebrating Achievements and Amplifying Strength: Rituals of Triumph

Womanist rituals offer a platform for celebrating individual and collective achievements. Graduations, career milestones, artistic accomplishments—these rituals acknowledge the successes that women of color have fought hard to attain. By highlighting triumphs, rituals amplify the strength and resilience that lie at the heart of womanist narratives.

Cultivating Community and Sisterhood: Rituals of Unity

Rituals become pivotal in forging connections and nurturing sisterhood among women of color. These gatherings, centered around shared practices and values, create spaces where individuals can authentically express themselves. Through rituals, women of color find solace, validation, and strength in the collective understanding of shared experiences and shared goals.

Fostering Resilience and Unity: Empowerment in Rituals

Womanist rituals not only celebrate achievements but also foster resilience. By collectively acknowledging challenges faced by women of color, rituals validate their struggles while underlining their capacity for overcoming adversity. These rituals nurture empowerment, reminding participants of their intrinsic worth and their shared capacity for transformation.

Rituals as Catalysts for Empowerment and Unity

As women of color gather to celebrate achievements, amplify strength, and nurture sisterhood through womanist rituals, they form a tapestry of empowerment that uplifts both individuals and the collective whole. These rituals provide spaces where success is celebrated, strength is magnified, and community is fortified. In the shared experience of rituals, womanists find a wellspring of empowerment that fuels their journey towards equality, justice, and liberation.

Cultural and Ancestral Connections: Reviving Power through Womanist Rituals

Let's dive into the profound significance of cultural and ancestral connections within womanist rituals. We explore how these rituals honor cultural heritage and indigenous knowledge, empowering women while challenging dominant narratives that have historically suppressed their voices.

Discussing Importance of Cultural Connections:

1. Reclaiming Identity: Cultural connections in womanist rituals are a means of reclaiming identity and agency, countering historical attempts at erasure.

2. Sustaining Traditions: By incorporating cultural practices, womanists sustain ancestral traditions that hold deep wisdom and spiritual significance.

Exploring Rituals that Honor Heritage:

1. Rituals of Resilience: Womanists create rituals that celebrate their cultural heritage, affirming their resilience and fostering a sense of belonging.

2. Indigenous Wisdom: Indigenous knowledge embedded in these rituals challenges dominant narratives, offering alternative perspectives on spirituality and womanhood.

Analyzing Empowerment through Connection:

1. Self-Empowerment: Cultural and ancestral connections in rituals empower women to embrace their authentic selves, fostering confidence and self-worth.

2. Counteracting Suppression: By challenging dominant narratives, womanists reshape the narrative landscape, centering their voices and experiences.

As we delve into the power of cultural and ancestral connections within womanist rituals, let us celebrate the ways in which these practices provide a space for empowerment, healing, and transformation. By engaging with and honoring their cultural heritage, womanists not only reaffirm their identities but also contribute to a broader movement for justice, equity, and spiritual liberation.

Rituals as Transformative Acts: Empowering Change with Womanist Practices

In this chapter, we delve into the profound transformative potential of womanist rituals for individuals and communities. We explore how these rituals challenge existing power structures and norms, while also fostering a sense of agency and empowerment among those who participate.

Examining Transformative Potential:

1. Personal Empowerment: Womanist rituals provide individuals with a space for personal growth, healing, and self-discovery, fostering a deeper connection to their identities.

2. Collective Resilience: Through communal participation, womanist rituals unite communities, fortifying them with a shared sense of purpose and strength.

Discussing Challenge to Power Structures:

1. Disrupting Norms: Womanist rituals challenge normative power structures by carving out spaces where individuals can redefine their relationship with spirituality and identity.

2. Reclaiming Authority: These rituals reclaim spiritual authority from institutions that have historically wielded it to suppress and control marginalized groups.

Highlighting Sense of Agency:

1. Fostering Empowerment: By actively participating in rituals, individuals gain a sense of agency over their spiritual journey, promoting a more empowered and authentic expression of faith.

2. Inspiring Action: Womanist rituals inspire individuals to take action beyond the ritual space, advocating for justice and equity in their broader communities.

As we explore the transformative nature of womanist rituals, let us embrace their potential to reshape our understanding of spirituality, foster resilience, and empower change. By engaging with these rituals, we tap into wellsprings of strength that challenge oppressive norms and pave the way for a more just and equitable world.

Inclusivity and Adaptability: Womanist Rituals Embrace Diversity

In this chapter, we delve into the remarkable inclusivity and adaptability of womanist rituals, highlighting their capacity to resonate across diverse contexts. We explore how these rituals accommodate various identities, experiences, and backgrounds, fostering a sense of belonging and empowerment. Additionally, we analyze the potential for cross-cultural exchanges and collaborations that enrich the womanist movement.

Discussing Inclusivity of Womanist Rituals:

1. Embracing All Identities: Womanist rituals intentionally create space for people of all genders, races, and backgrounds, acknowledging the intersectional nature of their experiences.

2. Breaking Down Barriers: By centering inclusivity, these rituals break down barriers that traditionally exclude marginalized voices, promoting a sense of unity and shared purpose.

Examining Adaptability to Diverse Contexts:

1. Fluid and Flexible: Womanist rituals adapt to diverse cultural, geographical, and contextual settings, ensuring their relevance and resonance across different communities.

2. Nurturing Individual Connections: The adaptability of these rituals allows individuals to connect with their spirituality in ways that align with their unique identities and journeys.

Analyzing Potential for Cross-Cultural Exchanges:

1. Cultural Exchange: Womanist rituals offer a platform for cross-cultural exchanges that facilitate the sharing of wisdom, traditions, and perspectives.

2. Collaborative Potential: Collaborations across cultures enrich the womanist movement, expanding its impact and fostering global solidarity for justice and equity.

As we navigate the inclusive and adaptable landscape of womanist rituals, let us celebrate the power of diversity and collaboration. By engaging with rituals that embrace our uniqueness and connect us across boundaries, we contribute to a vibrant and ever-evolving movement that seeks justice, equality, and transformation for all.

Conclusion: The Empowering Tapestry of Womanist Rituals

As we conclude our exploration into the world of womanist rituals, we find ourselves enveloped in a rich tapestry of empowerment, healing, and social change. Throughout this journey, we uncovered the remarkable inclusivity and adaptability of these rituals, their transformative potential, and their role in challenging religious norms.

Summarizing the Main Points:

From their role in fostering resilience to their power in reshaping spirituality, womanist rituals emerge as powerful tools for empowerment and social transformation.

Reflecting on the Significance:

The significance of womanist rituals lies in their capacity to challenge religious norms that have historically marginalized and excluded. They provide a space for healing, agency, and the celebration of diverse identities.

Encouraging Engagement and Creation:

As we reflect on the lessons of womanist rituals, let us embrace the invitation to engage with and even create our own rituals that promote healing, empowerment, and change. By weaving our stories into this ongoing tapestry, we contribute to a broader movement for justice, equity, and a spirituality that is inclusive and empowering for all.

As we move forward, may the wisdom of womanist rituals continue to inspire and guide us in our pursuit of a more just, equitable, and compassionate world.

Chapter 9: Pathways to Redemption: Womanism as Catalyst for Religious Transformation

Introduction: Womanism's Transformative Power in Religious Spaces

In this chapter, we delve into the remarkable potential of womanism as a catalyst for transforming religious spaces. We explore how womanist ideals, rooted in justice, equity, and inclusivity, have the power to challenge and reshape established religious institutions. By emphasizing the role of womanism in inspiring religious transformation, we unveil the journey toward greater inclusivity and justice within these spaces.

Womanism's Potential for Transformation:

1. Challenging Norms: Womanist ideals disrupt traditional norms that perpetuate exclusion and inequality within religious institutions.

2. Reimagining Paradigms: Womanism challenges religious spaces to reimagine their paradigms, embracing justice and inclusivity as central tenets.

Emphasizing Justice and Inclusivity:

1. The Call for Justice: Womanism calls religious institutions to uphold justice by dismantling oppressive structures and fostering environments of empowerment.

2. Pursuit of Inclusivity: Womanist ideals inspire religious spaces to embrace diverse voices, experiences, and identities, promoting true inclusivity.

As we embark on this exploration of womanism's transformative potential, let us recognize the power it holds to reshape religious spaces into bastions of justice, equity, and compassionate spirituality. Through womanism, we find a beacon of hope for a future where religious institutions serve as catalysts for positive change and inclusivity.

Challenging Religious Norms and Structures: Womanism's Subversive Influence

In this chapter, we delve into the integral role womanism plays in challenging established religious norms and structures. We explore how womanist values, firmly rooted in justice and equity, disrupt patriarchal and exclusionary practices that have historically characterized religious institutions. Through engagement with womanist perspectives, we unearth the potential for transformative evolution within these spaces.

Womanism's Disruption of Religious Norms:

1. A Paradigm Shift: Womanism prompts a paradigm shift by questioning and challenging the norms that perpetuate gender inequality, marginalization, and exclusion.

2. Demanding Accountability: Womanism holds religious institutions accountable for their complicity in sustaining oppressive structures, urging them to align with principles of justice.

Exploring Disruption of Patriarchal Practices:

1. Breaking Chains of Patriarchy: Womanist values challenge patriarchal practices that have limited women's roles, leadership, and contributions within religious contexts.

2. Expanding Boundaries: Womanism seeks to expand the boundaries of acceptable discourse, creating spaces for diverse voices and experiences to be heard and valued.

Highlighting Potential for Evolution:

1. Embracing Transformation: Religious institutions, through engagement with womanist perspectives, have the potential to evolve into spaces that actively promote justice, equality, and empowerment.

2. Shaping the Future: Womanism envisions a future where religious spaces embrace change, becoming catalysts for social progress and spiritual growth.

As we navigate the intersections of womanism and religious norms, let us celebrate the transformative potential inherent in challenging established practices. By engaging with womanist values, religious institutions can embark on a journey of self-reflection and transformation that aligns them with the principles of justice, equity, and inclusivity.

Reimagining Sacred Texts and Theologies: Womanism's Transformative Influence

Within the realm of womanism, sacred texts and theological interpretations undergo a process of reimagining that contributes to profound shifts in religious narratives. Womanism, with its emphasis on intersectionality and the experiences of women of color, brings fresh perspectives to the forefront, challenging traditional patriarchal interpretations and offering inclusive, equitable theological frameworks that resonate with the contemporary world.

The Power of Inclusivity in Theological Reimagining

Womanism's reimagining of sacred texts and theologies revolves around inclusivity and equity. Womanist scholars engage in a deliberate process of uncovering hidden narratives within religious texts that amplify the voices of women, particularly women of color. These reinterpretations resonate with the experiences of marginalized individuals and challenge oppressive norms, giving rise to theological frameworks that embrace the diversity and worth of all believers.

Transformative Potential of Equitable Theological Frameworks

By reimagining sacred texts and theologies, womanists carve a path toward transformation within religious communities. Equitable theological frameworks empower individuals who have been historically marginalized, enabling them to reclaim agency within their faiths. These frameworks provide a platform for addressing contemporary issues such as gender equality, LGBTQ+ inclusion, and social justice within the context of religious beliefs.

Engaging in Critical Dialogue and Reflection

Religious communities hold the potential to engage in critical dialogue and reflection, sparked by the reimagining efforts of womanism. Through open conversations, believers are encouraged to question traditional interpretations, challenge oppressive norms, and explore alternative perspectives. This dialogue cultivates a climate of growth and transformation, enabling religious traditions to evolve while remaining rooted in core values.

Womanism's Path to Transformation

As womanism reimagines sacred texts and theological interpretations, it ushers in a transformative era for religious communities. The power of inclusivity and equity resonates in these reimagined narratives, inspiring believers to confront oppressive norms and embrace a theology that reflects the complexity of human experiences. The potential for critical dialogue and reflection offers an avenue for growth, ensuring that religious traditions remain relevant and impactful in an ever-changing world. Womanism paves the way for a future where spirituality, justice, and empowerment intertwine harmoniously within the tapestry of faith.

Embracing Diverse Leadership and Representation: Womanism's Push for Change

Within the landscape of womanism, a powerful movement emerges that advocates for diverse leadership and representation within religious institutions. Womanists recognize that genuine progress toward equality and justice necessitates breaking free from traditional gender norms, challenging oppressive hierarchies, and fostering environments where a diverse range of voices can flourish.

The Significance of Representation in Challenging Gender Norms

Womanist efforts to promote diverse leadership directly challenge long-standing gender norms that have marginalized women within religious spaces. By occupying leadership roles, women of color disrupt preconceived notions of who can guide, teach, and inspire. Their presence shatters the glass ceiling, sending a resounding message that women can hold positions of authority and influence.

Inclusive Leadership's Impact on Just and Equitable Spaces

Inclusive leadership transforms religious spaces into platforms of justice and equity. When diverse perspectives guide decision-making, policies are formulated with a comprehensive understanding of the unique needs and experiences of all members. Inclusive leadership dismantles barriers that perpetuate discrimination, resulting in religious communities that genuinely reflect the values of compassion, empathy, and respect.

Empowering Future Generations: The Legacy of Diverse Leadership

Womanist efforts to promote diverse leadership transcend the present moment, leaving a legacy of empowerment for future generations. When young individuals witness women of color occupying leadership roles, they see possibilities beyond what tradition may dictate. This inspiration paves the way for a future where diverse leadership becomes the norm, challenging oppressive norms and fostering a more inclusive world.

The Transformative Power of Inclusive Leadership

As womanists champion diverse leadership and representation, they catalyze a transformation that reverberates throughout religious institutions. By challenging gender norms and advocating for equitable spaces, womanists forge a path toward a more just and compassionate world. In the embrace of inclusive leadership, religious communities evolve, embodying values that honor the dignity and worth of all individuals, regardless of their gender or background.

Fostering Inclusive Rituals and Practices: Womanism's Transformative Touch

Let's look into the transformative potential of womanist rituals within religious contexts. We explore how womanist rituals disrupt patriarchal and exclusive practices, breathing new life into religious spaces. Additionally, we highlight the significance of rituals that celebrate women's agency, voices, and experiences, paving the way for inclusive and empowering spiritual practices.

Womanist Rituals' Transformative Power:

1. Shifting Paradigms: Womanist rituals challenge established norms, inviting religious spaces to embrace practices that prioritize justice, equity, and inclusion.

2. Reclaiming Spirituality: These rituals serve as vehicles for reclaiming spirituality from patriarchal confines, allowing women to express their faith authentically.

Exploring Challenge to Patriarchal Practices:

1. Redefining Participation: Womanist rituals redefine participation, dismantling gendered hierarchies that have often marginalized women's contributions.

2. Embracing Diversity: By centering women's experiences, womanist rituals promote the recognition of diverse identities and stories within religious spaces.

Highlighting Celebratory Rituals:

1. Women's Agency: Womanist rituals celebrate women's agency and resilience, empowering them to fully engage with their faith journey.

2. Amplifying Voices: These rituals amplify women's voices and experiences, fostering a sense of belonging and validation within religious communities.

Interfaith and Intrafaith Dialogue

As we navigate the transformative landscape of womanist rituals, let us recognize the potential for rituals to reshape religious practices and spaces. By engaging with inclusive and celebratory rituals, we contribute to a more just, equitable, and vibrant spiritual landscape that honors the agency, voices, and experiences of all individuals.

Interfaith and Intrafaith Dialogue: Womanism's Bridge to Understanding

Womanism emerges as a bridge builder in both interfaith and intrafaith dialogue, creating spaces for conversations that center on gender equity, justice, and shared human experiences. With its emphasis on intersectionality and inclusivity, womanism enriches these dialogues by offering perspectives that challenge oppressive norms and inspire collaborations for positive change.

Contributing Womanist Perspectives to Gender Equity and Justice

Womanism injects fresh perspectives into interfaith and intrafaith dialogues surrounding gender equity and justice. By acknowledging the intersections of race, gender, and faith, womanists contribute nuanced viewpoints that uncover the complexities of oppression. Womanist perspectives shed light on the ways in which systems of power operate within religious contexts and inspire conversations that dismantle these hierarchies.

Fostering Cross-Faith Collaborations for Social Change

Cross-faith collaborations for social change become possible through womanist engagement in interfaith dialogue. Womanists recognize the common ground shared among various faith traditions in the pursuit of justice, equity, and human rights. By uniting across faith lines, womanists amplify their voices and create a powerful force for social transformation that transcends religious boundaries.

Nurturing Intrafaith Understanding and Empowerment

Intrafaith dialogue also finds a nurturing space within womanism. As women of color within the same faith tradition come together, they foster understanding, empathy, and shared empowerment. By sharing their unique experiences, struggles, and triumphs, womanists strengthen bonds within their own communities while challenging harmful practices that perpetuate gender inequality.

Womanism as Catalyst for Dialogue and Change

In the realm of interfaith and intrafaith dialogue, womanism emerges as a catalyst for meaningful conversations and transformative change. By bringing diverse perspectives to the table, womanists pave the way for cross-faith collaborations that address pressing issues of gender equity and justice. Through these dialogues, womanism demonstrates its potential to reshape religious landscapes, foster unity among women of color, and contribute to a world where faith becomes a force for positive social change.

The Ripple Effect: Womanism Beyond Religious Spaces

The influence of womanism transcends the confines of religious spaces, extending its reach to shape the social, political, and cultural landscapes. By advocating for justice, equity, and empowerment, womanism's principles reverberate through various contexts, igniting transformative movements that challenge oppressive norms and pave the way for a more inclusive and just world.

Womanist Principles and Their Broader Impact

Womanism's principles of intersectionality, inclusivity, and empowerment ripple outward, leaving an indelible mark on society. These principles challenge systems of oppression and address the multifaceted ways in which individuals experience discrimination. By embracing these values, womanism inspires individuals and communities to confront inequality and work toward systemic change.

Influence in Social, Political, and Cultural Arenas

In the social sphere, womanism influences advocacy efforts for gender equality, racial justice, and LGBTQ+ rights. By highlighting the experiences of women of color and underscoring the intersections of identity, womanism enriches discussions about social justice and shapes policies that address the unique challenges faced by marginalized communities.

In the political arena, womanism serves as a driving force behind movements that challenge discriminatory policies, amplify marginalized voices, and advocate for representation. Womanists mobilize communities to demand change and challenge political structures that perpetuate inequality.

In the cultural realm, womanism reshapes narratives in literature, art, and media, amplifying diverse voices and challenging stereotypical portrayals. By reclaiming cultural spaces and narratives, womanism disrupts harmful norms and fosters a more inclusive cultural landscape.

Inspiring Transformative Movements Across Contexts

The principles of womanism inspire movements that cross boundaries, uniting individuals from various backgrounds in pursuit of common goals. Whether it's racial justice, environmental advocacy, or economic equity, womanism provides a framework that invites diverse perspectives into the conversation and fosters collaborative action.

Womanism's Enduring Impact

The ripple effect of womanism extends far beyond religious spaces, shaping the way society addresses complex challenges. By embracing womanist principles, individuals and communities are empowered to challenge oppressive norms and work toward transformative change in social, political, and cultural spheres. Womanism's enduring impact lies in its ability to inspire collective action and create a more just and equitable world for all.

Conclusion: Empowering Transformation through Womanism

In this exploration of womanism's influence on religious institutions and beyond, we have delved into a tapestry of narratives, practices, and principles that redefines the landscape of faith, justice, and empowerment. Womanism's multifaceted strategies, rituals, and perspectives intersect to create a powerful force that challenges oppressive norms, reclaims spirituality, and fosters resilience. As we reflect on the potential for womanism to catalyze positive change within religious spaces, we are reminded of the profound impact it has on the broader world.

Main Points Revisited:

- Womanist narratives of resilience and triumph, highlighting real-life examples of women who defy religious constraints.
- Strategies for challenging oppressive religious norms, engaging in activism, and using theological arguments to challenge harmful beliefs.
- The reclamation of spiritual spaces through rituals and ceremonies that affirm womanist identities and foster healing.
- The significance of community building and mutual support, emphasizing collective action in challenging religious oppression.
- Educational initiatives, advocacy, and scholarly contributions that challenge traditional interpretations and promote inclusivity.
- The reimagining of sacred texts and theologies, fostering equitable frameworks and critical dialogue.
- The promotion of diverse leadership and representation within religious institutions, breaking free from gender norms.
- The role of womanism in interfaith and intrafaith dialogue, contributing to conversations about equity and justice.
- Womanism's impact beyond religious spaces, influencing social, political, and cultural arenas.

A Call to Engagement and Transformation:

As we conclude this chapter, let us not merely reflect, but engage. The potential for womanism to drive positive change within religious institutions is vast. By embracing womanist perspectives, we empower ourselves to challenge oppressive norms, advocate for inclusion, and foster resilience within our faith communities. Let us engage with womanism's principles and practices, seeking to transform our religious spaces into havens of justice, equality, and compassion. By joining the movement for change, we contribute to the creation of a more just and inclusive world—a world where womanism's influence echoes through the corridors of faith, inspiring transformation and embracing the power of all voices.

Chapter 10: Reconciliation and Renewal: Building Bridges Between Religion and Womanism

Introduction: Bridging Faith and Womanism

In the intricate dance between faith and womanism, lies a realm of possibility—of dialogue, reconciliation, and mutual understanding. This chapter delves into the journey of fostering connections between religion and womanism, exploring the potential for harmony and shared growth. As we embark on this exploration, we discover the significance of seeking common ground, building bridges, and nurturing spaces where faith and womanism coexist, inspiring transformative change in both spheres.

Reconciliation and Mutual Understanding: A Shared Horizon

At the heart of the intersection between religion and womanism lies the potential for reconciliation. While both domains have often been seen as polarities, they also share threads of commonality. This chapter illuminates the spaces where dialogue can flourish, forging connections that unravel misunderstandings and pave the way for mutual understanding. Through the lens of womanism, religious narratives find new dimensions of inclusivity, empathy, and shared empowerment.

Seeking Common Ground: Navigating Shared Values

Within the interplay of faith and womanism, common ground beckons—a place where shared values and aspirations converge. As we navigate this terrain, we uncover the possibilities for collaboration and growth that emerge when both religion and womanism recognize their shared commitment to justice, equity, and the liberation of marginalized voices. This chapter seeks to highlight these intersections, offering a vision of unity amidst diversity.

Creating Bridges: Channels of Transformation

The creation of bridges between religion and womanism becomes an act of transformation. These bridges facilitate the exchange of ideas, the sharing of stories, and the dismantling of barriers that have historically separated these spheres. In building these bridges, we craft pathways for collaboration, where the wisdom of faith and the empowerment of womanism harmoniously coexist, forging a brighter future for all.

A Journey of Discovery and Harmony

As we embark on this chapter's exploration, we embark on a journey of discovery—a journey that reveals the profound potential for dialogue, common ground, and bridge-building between religion and womanism. In seeking reconciliation, we illuminate the space where shared values flourish. By nurturing mutual understanding, we foster a world where faith and womanism complement and strengthen one another. This journey is a testament to the enduring capacity for growth, empathy, and transformation that lies at the intersection of these two dynamic realms.

Recognizing Shared Goals: A Confluence of Justice and Compassion

Within the realms of both religion and womanism, a shared undercurrent of goals emerges—goals that revolve around justice, compassion, and community. This chapter delves into the spaces where these shared aspirations intersect, and where the bridge between religion and womanism takes root, fostering dialogue and collaboration that resonate with the core of both traditions.

Common Values as the Basis for Dialogue: Uniting in Shared Principles

The foundation for fruitful dialogue lies in the common values that bind religion and womanism together. At their essence, both advocate for the upliftment of marginalized voices, the pursuit of equity, and the fostering of compassion. By recognizing these shared principles, a bridge is built, allowing for open conversations that acknowledge both the richness of faith and the empowerment of womanist perspectives.

Intersection of Religious Teachings and Womanist Principles: Commitment to Equity

The commitment to equity forms a nexus where religious teachings and womanist principles intersect. Religious texts often contain messages of justice and the care for the vulnerable. Womanism, with its focus on marginalized identities, amplifies these teachings, urging believers to challenge oppressive norms and create spaces where all are valued. This intersection presents an opportunity for dialogue that can illuminate the shared ground between faith and womanism.

A Unified Call for Justice: Bridging the Gap

The alignment of religious and womanist goals creates a unified call for justice—a call that beckons believers of all backgrounds to come together in collaborative action. By building bridges between these two spheres, we forge spaces where justice is not merely a concept, but a tangible force that reverberates through communities, transforming lives and bringing about positive change.

A Convergence of Values and Aspirations

In the exploration of shared goals between religion and womanism, we discover a convergence of values and aspirations that are rooted in justice, compassion, and community. By recognizing these shared principles, we carve out spaces for dialogue, collaboration, and transformation. As religious teachings and womanist principles intersect in their commitment to equity, they unite to form a powerful call for justice that transcends the boundaries of tradition, embracing a vision of a more inclusive and compassionate world for all.

Challenges and Tensions: Navigating the Intersections of Religion and Womanism

In this chapter, we acknowledge the complexities that arise when attempting to reconcile religion and womanism. We openly discuss the areas of conflict and disagreement that emerge as these two forces intersect. By exploring these challenges and tensions, we uncover the potential for deeper understanding and growth.

Acknowledging Conflicts and Disagreements:

1. Traditional Beliefs: The clash between patriarchal religious teachings and womanist values can lead to conflicts regarding gender roles and equality.

2. Scriptural Interpretations: Divergent interpretations of sacred texts often lead to tensions over the role of women in religious contexts.

Exploring Areas of Conflict:

1. Leadership Roles: Disagreements arise over the extent to which women can hold leadership positions within religious institutions.

2. Moral and Ethical Frameworks: Conflicting moral and ethical perspectives on issues such as reproductive rights can strain the relationship between religion and womanism.

Acknowledging for Deeper Understanding:

1. Dialogue as Catalyst: Acknowledging these tensions provides an opportunity for dialogue that fosters empathy and encourages critical reflection.

2. Nuanced Perspectives: Engaging with areas of conflict allows for a nuanced understanding of both religion and womanism, leading to a more well-rounded perspective.

As we navigate the challenges and tensions at the crossroads of religion and womanism, let us recognize that open and honest discussions can lead to greater understanding and transformation. By addressing these complexities, we pave the way for a more inclusive and harmonious intersection between these two integral aspects of individuals' lives.

Open Dialogue and Intersectionality: Bridging Divides through Understanding

In this chapter, we delve into the significance of open and respectful dialogue between religious and womanist perspectives. We emphasize how intersectionality, with its focus on the interconnected nature of identities and experiences, plays a pivotal role in fostering understanding and unity. By exploring these dynamics, we uncover how intersectional approaches enrich both religious and womanist worldviews.

Importance of Open Dialogue:

1. Building Bridges: Open dialogue promotes mutual respect and empathy between religious and womanist perspectives, fostering a space for meaningful exchange.

2. Breaking Stereotypes: Dialogue challenges stereotypes and misconceptions, paving the way for a deeper grasp of the complexities inherent in both approaches.

Emphasizing Intersectionality:

1. Interconnected Identities: Intersectionality recognizes that identities are interconnected, leading to shared experiences that can bridge gaps between different perspectives.

2. Fostering Empathy: Understanding intersectionality nurtures empathy, as individuals recognize the overlapping struggles and aspirations that unite us all.

Enriching Worldviews:

1. Religious Insights: Intersectional approaches can broaden religious perspectives by incorporating a deeper understanding of the diverse lived experiences of believers.

2. Deepening Womanist Values: An intersectional lens enhances womanist values by recognizing the multiple layers of identity and experience that shape the movement.

As we explore open dialogue and intersectionality, let us embrace the opportunity to bridge divides, deepen empathy, and enrich our collective understanding of the intricate interplay between religious and womanist perspectives. By recognizing our shared humanity and embracing our diverse identities, we contribute to a more inclusive and harmonious world.

Education and Awareness: Illuminating Pathways to Understanding

In this chapter, we embark on a journey into the role of education in fostering dialogue between religion and womanism. We delve into how awareness campaigns, workshops, and resources serve as illuminating tools, paving the way for deeper understanding and empathy. By exploring these avenues, we uncover the potential for education to dispel misconceptions and facilitate harmonious engagement.

The Role of Education in Dialogue:

1. Knowledge as Catalyst: Education serves as a catalyst for meaningful dialogue, empowering individuals with the information needed for informed and respectful conversations.

2. Creating Common Ground: Education provides a shared foundation of awareness, enabling both religious and womanist perspectives to engage more effectively.

Importance of Awareness Campaigns:

1. Challenging Stereotypes: Awareness campaigns challenge stereotypes and prejudices, revealing the multifaceted nature of religious and womanist ideals.

2. Fostering Empathy: These campaigns inspire empathy by shedding light on the shared struggles and aspirations that bridge the gap between perspectives.

Workshops and Resources as Empowering Tools:

1. Facilitating Engagement: Workshops offer safe spaces for open dialogue, allowing individuals to ask questions, share experiences, and learn from one another.

2. Dispelling Misconceptions: Resources provide accurate information, dispelling misconceptions that may hinder constructive dialogue.

Potential for Empathy and Understanding:

1. Dispelling Myths: Education equips individuals with the tools to challenge and dispel myths that fuel misunderstandings.

2. Fostering Empathy: As education nurtures empathy, individuals can approach conversations with a genuine desire to understand and connect.

As we navigate the pathways of education and awareness, let us recognize their potential to bridge divides and foster empathy between religion and womanism. By investing in knowledge and engaging with open hearts and minds, we create an environment where fruitful dialogue can flourish, paving the way for a more harmonious and inclusive coexistence.

Reimagining Religious Spaces: Embracing Inclusivity and Change

In this chapter, we delve into strategies for transforming religious spaces into havens of inclusivity and welcome. We explore the ways in which patriarchal norms within religious communities can be challenged and replaced with womanist principles. By exploring successful examples, we uncover the potential for religious institutions to embrace positive change.

Strategies for Transformation:

1. Inclusive Leadership: Fostering diverse leadership ensures that various voices, including those of women and marginalized groups, are represented and valued.

2. Reimagining Rituals: Introducing inclusive rituals that celebrate agency, equality, and diverse identities reshapes the spiritual landscape.

Challenging Patriarchal Norms:

1. Educative Initiatives: Educational programs and workshops can challenge patriarchal norms by raising awareness and fostering critical reflection.

2. Redefining Scriptures: Engaging in reinterpretation efforts allows for a fresh understanding of religious texts that align with equity and justice.

Successful Examples of Change:

1. Women's Leadership: Highlighting cases where women assume leadership roles challenges traditional norms and paves the way for inclusivity.

2. Inclusive Liturgy: Successful stories of religious communities embracing inclusive language and liturgy can inspire similar transformations.

By exploring strategies for change, we take a step toward reimagining religious spaces as hubs of inclusivity, equity, and transformation. Let us celebrate these successful examples and draw inspiration from them to create religious communities that embody womanist principles, fostering a more just and harmonious spiritual experience for all.

Collaborative Projects: Harnessing Collective Power for Change

In this chapter, we delve into the potential collaborative projects between religious and womanist communities. We explore initiatives that tackle social justice, gender equity, and community development, uniting these two movements toward shared goals. By analyzing the impact of collaboration, we uncover the strength that arises when collective efforts are harnessed for positive change.

Exploring Collaborative Projects:

1. Social Justice Advocacy: Joint initiatives focusing on systemic change, addressing issues like poverty, racial inequality, and gender-based violence, can drive impactful social justice outcomes.

2. Gender Equity Initiatives: Collaborative efforts to challenge gender norms and empower women within religious contexts can foster a more inclusive spiritual environment.

Addressing Community Needs:

1. Community Development: Joint projects that uplift marginalized communities, regardless of religious or womanist affiliation, create a platform for unity and progress.

2. Empowerment Programs: Collaborative initiatives can offer workshops, training, and resources that empower individuals to lead meaningful and self-determined lives.

Amplifying Impact through Collaboration:

1. Intersectional Advocacy: Collaborative projects inherently embrace intersectionality, acknowledging the multifaceted nature of challenges faced by individuals.

2. Amplified Voices: When religious and womanist communities join forces, their collective voices amplify the message of justice and equity, reaching a wider audience.

By exploring collaborative projects, we celebrate the potential for shared efforts to ignite positive change. Let us embrace the spirit of unity and collaboration, working together to build a world where religious and womanist ideals converge to create a more just, equitable, and harmonious society for all.

Conclusion: Bridging the Gap between Religion and Womanism

In this concluding chapter, we reflect on the journey we've taken, summarizing the key points that have illuminated the complex and enriching relationship between religion and womanism. We recognize the potential for building bridges and finding common ground between these two realms, fostering understanding and transformative change.

Summarizing the Main Points:

1. Intersectionality's Power: We explored how intersectionality lies at the heart of womanism, enabling inclusive conversations that challenge gender norms, racial biases, and religious inequalities.

2. Reimagining Religious Spaces: We discussed strategies for transforming religious spaces into inclusive havens, where womanist principles can flourish alongside spiritual practices.

3. Collaborative Momentum: We uncovered the potential for collaborative projects to amplify the impact of both religious and womanist communities, fostering social change and gender equity.

Reflecting on Possibilities:

By understanding the intersection of religion and womanism, we open pathways for dialogue and unity that can reshape religious institutions and enrich womanist ideals. As we reflect on these possibilities, we recognize the potential for personal transformation and collective empowerment.

Embracing Transformative Change:

As we conclude this exploration, we encourage you, the reader, to engage in open dialogue, seek understanding, and contribute to the transformative change that both religion and womanism can offer. By joining the conversation, fostering empathy, and embracing the principles of justice and equity, we pave the way for a world where the intersection of religion and womanism creates a tapestry of shared values, diverse perspectives, and harmonious coexistence.

Chapter 11: Forward Together: Envisioning an Inclusive Future

Introduction: Envisioning an Inclusive Future of Unity

In this chapter, we turn our gaze toward envisioning an inclusive future that seamlessly integrates the values of religion and womanism. We delve into the vast potential for collaboration and progress, working hand in hand to forge a society that embodies justice, equity, and unity. With our eyes fixed on this collective vision, we emphasize the significance of looking ahead and working collaboratively to bring about positive change.

A Unified Vision of Inclusivity:

1. A Tapestry of Values: The integration of religious and womanist principles paints a tapestry that weaves together justice, compassion, and empowerment.

2. Bridging Divides: Envisioning an inclusive future requires us to bridge the gaps between different perspectives and values.

Collaboration for Positive Change:

1. Shared Goals: Collaboration between religion and womanism creates an avenue for shared goals, fostering a world that upholds gender equity, social justice, and harmony.

2. Amplified Impact: The combined efforts of religious and womanist communities amplify the impact of initiatives aiming to create a more just and equitable society.

The Road Ahead:

1. Collective Responsibility: As we look ahead, it's imperative to recognize that achieving an inclusive future is a collective responsibility that transcends individual boundaries.

2. Harmonious Coexistence: By working together, we lay the foundation for a future where individuals from diverse religious and womanist backgrounds coexist harmoniously, celebrating their shared values.

With our sights set on this inclusive future, let us move forward with determination, commitment, and an unwavering belief in the potential for positive change. By embracing collaboration and nurturing a spirit of unity, we can build a world that embraces justice, gender equity, and a rich tapestry of diverse perspectives.

Acknowledging Progress and Challenges: A Path of Reflection

As we reflect on the journey of promoting dialogue between religion and womanism, we acknowledge the progress that has been made in fostering understanding and unity. Yet, we also recognize the continued challenges and barriers that persist. By acknowledging both progress and challenges, we inform future strategies, ensuring that our efforts remain focused, effective, and responsive to evolving needs.

Intersectionality as a Guiding Principle: Embracing Unity in Diversity

Intersectionality emerges as a guiding principle for an inclusive future. By recognizing the interconnectedness of various forms of oppression, we pave the way for holistic solutions that transcend individual struggles. This approach benefits both religious and womanist perspectives, as it fosters a deeper understanding of shared struggles and collaborative solutions that uplift all.

Cultivating Empathy and Understanding: Seeds of Unity

Cultivating empathy and understanding becomes paramount in our journey toward an inclusive future. Active listening and seeking common ground create bridges between differing viewpoints, encouraging productive dialogue. Empathy, as a powerful force, can bridge gaps and create space for transformative conversations that shape our collective path forward.

Youth and Future Generations: Architects of Change

Youth and future generations hold a pivotal role in shaping an inclusive future. Their fresh perspectives and unwavering commitment to breaking down religious and gender-based barriers propel us toward progress. By providing education and platforms for young voices, we empower them to contribute to a world that embodies justice, equity, and unity.

Inclusive Religious Education: Building a Foundation for Change

Promoting inclusive religious education becomes a cornerstone for our shared vision. By revising teachings and curricula to be more equitable, religious institutions pave the way for transformative change within their communities. Education emerges as a powerful tool that can reshape attitudes, dismantle stereotypes, and foster mutual respect.

Advocacy for Policy Change: Enacting Tangible Transformation

Collaborative advocacy for policy change presents a path toward tangible transformation. When religious and womanist communities unite their efforts, they address systemic inequalities at the core. Engaging with policy makers and advocating for change translates ideals into practical actions that uplift marginalized groups and create lasting impact.

As we navigate this intricate journey, let us draw strength from our achievements and face challenges with resilience. By embracing intersectionality, empathy, the wisdom of youth, inclusive education, and advocacy, we create a roadmap for an inclusive future where religion and womanism converge to build a world marked by unity, justice, and equity.

Conclusion: Forging Connections Beyond Belief

As we reach the end of this exploration at the crossroads of religion and womanism, we find ourselves immersed in a unique journey—one that bridges the perspectives of atheism and empowerment. In tracing the intricate interplay of these seemingly divergent paths, we have unveiled a narrative of strength, resilience, and unity that transcends the confines of belief systems.

Discovering Common Ground: Embracing Shared Values

While this book's exploration may be anchored in an humanistic perspective, it also delves into shared values that extend beyond religious boundaries. The principles of empowerment, justice, compassion, and inclusivity serve as bridges connecting individuals across various belief systems. These shared values become the foundation upon which dialogue, understanding, and collaboration can flourish.

Embracing Empowerment Beyond Belief

At the heart of this exploration lies a celebration of empowerment, a force that is not confined to any particular belief system. Womanism's emphasis on empowerment and liberation resonates universally, inspiring individuals to challenge oppression, uplift marginalized voices, and create spaces that honor human dignity. This celebration underscores the potential for empowerment to transcend religious labels and become a beacon of positive change.

Shaping an Inclusive Future: Your Role in the Narrative

The journey we've embarked upon does not end with the book's conclusion—it continues within the lives and actions of each reader. As you reflect on the intersections of equity, empowerment, and shared values, envision your role in shaping a more inclusive future. By fostering dialogue, advocating for justice, and engaging in collaboration, you contribute to a world where individuals from diverse backgrounds find common ground and work together for positive transformation.

Empowerment Beyond Belief: A Legacy of Change

Ultimately, this book's exploration underscores the potential for empowerment to transcend the boundaries of belief. It demonstrates that empowerment is not limited to religious or non-religious frameworks—it is a force that can be harnessed by all individuals seeking to create a more just, compassionate, and equitable world. As you carry the insights gained from this exploration into your own life, you become a part of a legacy that champions empowerment beyond belief, inspiring change that knows no bounds.

A Call to Action: Empowerment Unites Us All

In closing this chapter, remember that empowerment is a force that unites us all, regardless of our belief systems. It transcends divisions and invites us to collaborate in building a better future. As you step forward, let empowerment guide your actions, conversations, and advocacy. In doing so, you contribute to a tapestry of positive change that encompasses individuals from all walks of life, fostering a world where empowerment becomes a universal language of transformation.